Praise for *Even*

"*Even So* is a rich, loving, and irreverent description of a chaotic and resilient family: both a snapshot of a quickly receding past and a celebration of a family that both splinters and regenerates over time. This is a dazzling, spellbinding book, as heart-wrenching as it is uplifting and whimsical. A must-read."—**Douglas Trevor**, author, *Girls I Know*

"Punctuated by the surreal and often devastating turns of fate that come with growing up in a large family on a working farm, *Even So* is funny, dark, and deeply moving. Written with startling frankness and heaps of compassion, this memoir is a nourishing read for anyone with a difficult family history. This book represents a reckoning—it does heavy emotional work and yet somehow shares this with us as if it were a great adventure. *Even So* is a celebration of the resilience of a gay kid and a loving portrait of a family in all its flaws."—**Jennifer Doyle**, author, *Hold it Against Me*

"About halfway through *Even So*, David Coster tells us that 'a surgeon can't be a surgeon if they feel too much at the wrong time.' Well, this book feels too much at exactly the right time. It's as if Coster has found a way to operate on life itself—in that theatre we call memory. Eudora Welty would have loved this richly fashioned Iowa farmhouse memoir."—**Ralph James Savarese**, author, *See It Feelingly* and *When This Is Over*

"For everyone who has felt out of place—or in a place that might seem out of place for others—this is a book to read: lovely, cherished and thoughtful connections."
—**Tama Janowitz**, author, *Slaves of New York*

"Reading *Even So* is like leafing through a family photo album. Each chapter of David Coster's memoir is a snapshot of the pleasures, difficulties, and occasional tragedies of life on an Iowa farm in the second half of the twentieth century. Collectively, they tell the story of Coster's struggle to move beyond the limited expectations of his strict father and fundamentalist mother to claim his own identity as father, surgeon, and gay man. I found this to be a moving and unexpectedly compelling book, written with insight, clarity, and precision."—**Stephen McCauley**, author, *My Ex-Life*

"By turns heart-stopping, soul-warming, and hilarious, *Even So* is an achievement up there with our most treasured tributes to heartland life. It has the hard-won wisdom gained only through great hardship and true happiness. Such vivid, loving insight is truly rare, and David Coster delivers it with a true sense of good story. His family farmstead teems with unforgettable characters, striking adventures, and poignant struggles—a world rich with life's most necessary realities."
—**Jesse Matz** (John Crowe Ransom Professor of English, Kenyon College), author, *The Modern Novel: A Short Introduction*

"Raw, vulnerable, and sincere, David Coster's *Even So* is a memoir that stays with you days after you finish the last page. Swept up in the lush language and the ever-evolving lives of Coster and his family, I found myself itching to read 'just one more page' over and over. This book is an absolute gem."—**Michael Leali**, author, *The Civil War of Amos Abernathy and Matteo*

"David Coster's big-hearted and keenly observed memoir of his rural queer childhood in 1960s Iowa is a moving reminder of life in the last century, and a window into

those parts of American culture that have risen to prominence in recent years. *Even So* is raw, funny, tragic, and, ultimately, hopeful–just what we all need!"
—**Andrea Lawlor**, author, *Paul Takes the Form of a Mortal Girl*

"David Coster paints a vivid, engaging, and ultimately deep and moving picture of a childhood that almost seems like fiction—growing up in a rural Iowa farm family whose days seem plucked from *The Waltons* or even another century. When tragedy strikes amid the adventures, the stresses and longings beneath the bucolic setting come to the surface and give Coster his primary themes of overcoming loss and obstacles, what we can escape and what we can't. *Even So* tells a life story that maps, with extraordinary recall of details and honest and humane insights, a doctor's and dad's particular journey, pointing the way to forgiveness, kindness, and the universal hope that, despite disappointments, the next chapter, the next generation, will be better."—**Evan Wolfson**, author, *Why Marriage Matters: America, Equality, and Gay People's Right to Marry*

"Autobiography is too turgid a word for this extraordinary memoir. Its intimate matter-of-factness drew me in so thoroughly that it was as though any world I might have lived in apart from it dropped away. Every lambent detail, each finely drawn commentary as seen through a child's wise, wry wit opened up a world that was brilliantly tender and so exquisitely brutal that I began reinhabiting my own scenes of childhood, wondering how David Coster might have dwelled in them, how he might have shown me the path to speak them, and revise them through compassion. Weaving the ordinariness of rural family life in Iowa in the 1960s and 1970s into domestic, local, and transnational histories through vignettes composed in dense mises-en-scène which lay bare the quirks of cruelty and mischance, *Even So* gifts readers the nuances of possibility tucked into curiosity, play, humor, desire, and kindness, leavened constantly with longing, hope, and extraordinary courage. It is no accident that David Coster is a surgeon who has given his being over to healing—this is what he grants us through his memoir. *Even So* is not just a primer for any of us who have had childhoods pummeled into submission. Rather, it stands as a living allegory of our times, almost homeopathic, something we can turn to as we read the news to recoup a life out of the pieces of virulence that have become our collective histories."—**Geeta Patel**, author, *Unforeseen Poet: How I Found Myself in Lyric* and *Risky Bodies & Techno-Intimacy: Reflections on Sexuality, Media, Science, Finance*

EVEN SO

STORIES FROM AN
OVERPOPULATED FARMHOUSE

David D. Coster

Ice Cube Press, LLC
North Liberty, Iowa, USA

Dedication

This book is dedicated to my sons, Adam, Seth, and Sam, who healed me and made me whole again; to my nine siblings, who all have their own truths and stories to tell; to my mom, who did the best she could and kept her sanity — at least mostly; to my dad, whom I loved and despaired about; to my former wife, Julie, with whom I shared twenty wonderful years; and to my husband Kevin, who stirred my soul and awakened me to the whole wide world.

"I love Mom because she lets me go outdoors. I like a cowboy story better than I do my mom. She makes me go to bed and she spanks me if I don't. One day I got into some candy and she spanked me and then she gave me some candy herself. One day I sneaked outdoors and she spanked me outdoors. I get spanked all the time. Another time I sneaked up the apple tree and she spanked me then too. One time I brought a cat and kitten in the house and I put the kitten in a small dollhouse and it couldn't breathe and it died and I got a bad spanking from both Dad and Mom. One day I got into Mom's knives and got a knife and cut up a yellow box that Mom needed real bad and I got a bad spanking. I am a little devil!"*

—*Neal Coster, 1961, age 3.*

"Mom is pretty good. I never get spanked, I'm so good. One time my daddy was out at the hog house and he brought a kitten in the house and Mom thought I had done it and she spanked me instead of Daddy. My mom is sometimes a big devil."*

—*Mary Ann Coster, 1961, age 4.*

*As recorded by the hand of Grandma Coster, age 75.

TABLE OF CONTENTS ———

PART ONE

☙

PART TWO

✧

PART ONE

CORA'S ROOM ────────────

One day, when I was three, Dad told me to go wake up Great-aunt Cora. So, I padded barefoot down the green-tiled hall-way to her room. It was early, and the sun was streaming through the picture window of Mom and Dad's bedroom, and along nearly the entire length of the hall. I looked at the sun glinting off the wispy black and white patterns in the green linoleum squares as I trudged along, eventually reaching up to turn the brass knob on the smooth birch bedroom door.

I hesitated.

I hated going in there. The room smelled of old ladies, that nose-clogging smell of too-strong perfume and old urine. It was packed in an unsightly way with gobs of things that no one in their right mind would keep: old magazines, broken hair brushes, trinkets, and junk.

Aunt Cora's stringy hair was piercing white, her skin pale and translucent. I could see it all from the door, glowing in the early morning half-light. I was scared. The blue of her veins snaked about in stark contrast to the whiteness of her skin. Her wheelchair, in which she sat watching me with her watery blue eyes each day as I played in the living room, sat uselessly in the corner. A stroke had left her speechless, and helplessly stuck in that chair, so stuck, in fact, that Dad every day had to drag her out of it and plop her on the toilet just so she could go to the bathroom. Her bowels wouldn't work, so he'd knead her belly like a big lump of dough, pushing and punching until something finally came out of her. It was painful, and she'd moan and squirm, but it had to be done. And Dad would get mad after a while if it took too long, getting more and more irritated and rough as the moments went by, grossed out I suppose to be doing such a disgusting thing. If I watched too long, he would eventually start yelling at me too, so I only saw it a couple of times. Then he'd have to wipe her white ass, the bathroom smelling to high heaven by then, and somehow put her clothes back on, all lopsided, and put her back into the wheelchair, where I think she was crying, but who would know with such watery eyes? She was ancient – over ninety.

I approached her cast iron bed with the beat-up old mattresses and rag quilt, gingerly stepping around her various things strewn about, and climbed up on the side, hanging onto the mattress for leverage. I stared. Geez, she smelled bad. I shook her shoulder quickly and told her to "wake up!" but she just laid there. No sound. Her nose hairs were poking out, I noticed, long enough to be braided if anyone was interested. I pushed on her face. Her skin was oddly stiff and unusually cold. I poked her harder in the cheek, my finger meeting unusual resistance. Nothing happened. I stared at her some more. I looked in her ear. I told her to wake up again. Nothing happened.

I decided she was dead.

I climbed off the mattress and hightailed it to Dad's room, running right past him with my chubby legs as he stood by the closet in his underwear, looking for his overalls. I spun around on the parquet floor on my bare feet. "I can't get Aunt Cora up! She's dead!" I blurted out, my blue eyes wide.

Dad turned and looked at me a moment, studying my face, his overalls hanging slack in his hands, one buckle scraping the floor. I couldn't tell if he believed me or not. His piercing blue eyes looked hard back into my own like a mirror, searching for any sign of lying. My chest heaved as I tried to catch my breath. Dad decided I was serious. "She is, is she?!" he finally said with a look of concerned amusement. I began jumping up and down; for a moment, I'd thought I might merely be dismissed as an idiot.

"Hurry up! She's dead, I'm telling you! I'm sure of it!" I raced down the hall, in my shorts, Dad following in his underwear, to inspect what I had found. I leaped onto the bed and with immense relief found she hadn't moved a smidgeon. "See! See! She's dead!" Dad walked up and studied her, touched her, looked at her eyes, and watched for a few seconds.

"I'll be darned, you're right. She IS dead!"

I stared at her for a moment, watching each crease in her face, waiting for something to happen. Dad was quiet, just looking. Suddenly, I reached up and propped open an eye. I couldn't help it. "Can she see the fire alarm?" I asked.

"No! She can't see the fire alarm, you nitwit! She's dead!" Dad glared at me, irritation oozing into his face and voice. "So, what," I chirped. "Her eye's open, so she should be able to see it. She's looking right at it, can't you see that, Dad?"

Dad's hand snaked down like a water moccasin and smacked me a good one on the back of the head, an unexpected blow out of nowhere. "Don't be so damned ridiculous! Everyone knows dead people can't see, even if you open their eyes! Good gawd, you dumb kid! Now get the hell out of here and go find your mother."

I ran bawling down the hall, and took a sharp right into

the living room, running blindly to the kitchen to find my mom, my heels skimming over the purple and green of the swirling flowers imbedded in the short gray carpet; past the red and black couch with all the stuffing coming out from my jumping on it, then past the ebony upright piano with its glistening white keys, and finally over the cold white dining room linoleum and onto the blue of the kitchen floor – both floors with that same black and white twirling hallway pattern lazing along on the surface, making misty clouds and animals and soldiers going to war – and finally I was safe; there she was.

"What's the matter?" Mom asked, throwing a dish towel over her shoulder, turning from the sink where she was, as usual, washing up a few dishes. She pushed a wisp of curly brown hair away from her glasses and looked down at me, lips pursed.

"Aunt Cora's dead," I bawled, "and I found her, and Dad just hit me in the head and told me to get out of there just because I asked a question!" I continued to bawl.

"Are you kidding?" Mom replied. "Aunt Cora's dead?"

"Yeah, she's dead. And I found her!" I bawled, irritated that even Mom failed to recognize my importance just then. All anybody seemed to care about was that Cora was dead, not that I was the one who figured it out. Where was my reward? Would someone please tell me what a smart boy I was for finding her and figuring out she was dead? I bawled some more.

"Here, I'll pour you a bowl of cereal," Mom said, grabbing a bowl and filling it with Cheerios. She slopped on some milk and shoved in a spoon, wadding and throwing down the dishtowel at the same time. "You just stay here while I go see what's going on."

"I want to go too!" I yelled. "I'm the one who found her!"

"You just stay put, young man. If she's dead, it's no place for little kids to be playing around. Now sit back down and eat your cereal like I told you to."

So, I sat there and sulked, head in hands, glaring at my cereal and wondering what they were doing back there in Cora's room. I overheard a lot of chatter. "Better call the funeral home...don't forget to call your sister, Johnny...make sure the kids stay out of there...what are we going to do with all this stuff...better keep the door closed until they get here..." I sat there bawling until my cereal was soggy.

Eventually, I snuck back into the living room and lurked by the couch until Mom and Dad marched off to take care of something, then silently slipped back into Cora's room and climbed up again to stare, holding my breath. I touched her again, running my fingers down the length of her stiff arm, wondering what was going on inside of there, why she couldn't move, why she couldn't see, why she seemed frozen, locked in this hideous body on a cold mattress in a cluttered room. I opened her eye again, looking around to make sure Dad wasn't coming down the hall. It was like dull glass, like the eye of an old doll.

What was "dead," anyway? What, really, had happened to make her stop working? And then the air burst out of my lungs, and I had to run out and get some more. Mom and Dad came back just then, and I couldn't get caught hiding there in the hallway, so I ran into their bedroom and lay on their bed, staring at the closet and listening to their occasional murmurs behind the door of Cora's room.

After a bit, there was a strong knock on the front door. I leapt from Mom and Dad's bed and raced to the dining room to see what was happening next, my anger temporarily for-gotten. They answered it together, pushing me aside as they greeted the two men standing there in the snow. I hid behind Mom, watching them closely as they came in and stood be-side the giant closet separating the entryway from the living room. I had never seen such men: tall, broad-shouldered, fine-ly combed black hair under fine hats, nice teeth, kind eyes, smooth faces, chiseled jaws. They were shockingly handsome in their long black cloaks, and very respectful to Mom and Dad, shaking their hands and speaking calmly in deep voic-es upon entering the room. I was mesmerized, noticing their powerful gloved hands and the way their coats hung effort-lessly over their shoulders, outlining the shapes of their pow-erful chests and arms underneath; the timbre of their voices seemed to melt me. And the smell of them — what was that? That delicious smell, like perfume, but better. It went in my nose and then my whole body; my stomach tingled, and I was blinded by desire for those big, dark men, drawn in like a comet wandering too close to the sun. I wanted to be picked up by their big arms, wrapped in their cloaks, and carried away, safely snuggled inside with my little face buried in the heat of their chests, their arms crushing me, and smelling that oh-so-delicious smell! I stood staring at them, frozen, yet burning up.

And then, one looked at me, took off his hat, leaned down and touched me on the chin. "Hi, little guy," he said. He smiled. He smelled even better from this distance. I was too smitten to speak. He looked at me for a moment. He had a dimple. And then he was up and gone, turning on his heel, his black cloak following him into Cora's room.

I watched from the safety of the couch as those two men

hauled Aunt Cora out of the house, on a skinny bed with steel legs on wheels, covered with a white sheet. They struggled to get the bed around the hallway corners, their wool coats flapping and interfering as they strained. The entrance from the hallway to the living room had an odd sort of zigzag to accommodate the cupboards and shelves Mom needed for her little library of schoolbooks and World Book Encyclopedias. Plus, the toybox sat right there. It all made for architectural interest and a good hiding place, but it was lousy for getting dead bodies out of the house, and the handsome men weren't any too agile about it. First, they banged into one wall with Aunt Cora, and then another, and then the wheels caught on the carpet, and her feet jammed into the bookcase, and so on until they eventually broke her loose, finally, pausing only for a moment of last-minute instructions to Mom and Dad before hauling her out the front door, bouncing unceremoniously down the steps and disappearing in a veil of heavily falling snow.

Mom went and sat in the rocking chair in the living room, brow knit, rocking slowly. I crawled onto her lap. My bare feet were cold.

"I think I'll put you and Neal in Aunt Cora's room, David. Maybe I'll get you two a nice little set of bunk beds. Yeah, that would be nice. There's plenty of room in there for a nice set of bunk beds..."

"NO!" I hollered. "There's a ghost in there! It'll get me! I'm not sleeping in there! And I won't get in that horrible bed! It stinks in there!"

"Oh, for heaven's sake, David, we'll clean it all up and get you two boys *new* beds, and it'll be just fine! We'll throw away the old bed. And besides, there's no such thing as a ghost!

Now quit being so silly. You can stay in your own toddler bed for a while until we get it done and ready for you two anyway. It'll be awful nice to have the extra room."

I snuggled further into her lap. Maybe Mom was right; the ghost, if still there now, would probably be gone pretty soon. But I liked sleeping in the nursery right beside Mom, where I could see her, and Cora's room was all the way down the hall, clear at the other end! If her ghost did come, Mom would never hear my screams in time to save me.

I was getting sleepy. I snuggled in further. "Mom?" "What, David."

"I want the top bunk."

LITTLE BOYS AND
BLACK EYES

I have an unusual memory for detail, and it started early. I studied everything I saw, and reported my findings to Mom continuously. She found this quite amusing, and often asked me to go with her to work in the garden or do other chores around the house, or even go to town with her to look at fabrics for new shirts and dresses, which she sewed by hand. I kept her entertained with tales of cricket behavior in the strawberry patch, or regaled her with minute details of the growth patterns of feathers in baby birds I fished out of nests all over the farm. I was a little Tarzan, a nature boy who was happiest barefoot and nearly naked, climbing trees or exploring creek-banks populated with songbirds, and frogs and toads. I frequently spent entire days wandering the fields and meadows in search of interesting things for my collections, climbing trees to eat mulberries, and sucking water from field tiles to stay alive. It seemed like a game to me. From a distance, I might hear Mom ringing the old school bell on top of the garage to tell me it was time for lunch, but sometimes I was just too busy and too far away to make it. Eventually, I would show up, happy and covered with dust and bug bites from my travels in the Iowa "bush," with new material for my reports to my beloved mother.

Mom (Eleanor Ann Felsing) grew up near Laurens, Iowa, a small farming community that eighty-eight years later is still just the same small farming community with different faces in it, many with the same family names that have been there for generations. She was a Felsing (German origin: Voelsing, or Voltzing). The ancestral Felsing family started a clock company in Germany's Black Forest in the 1700s and eventually moved to Berlin, where the company, the Conrad Felsing Clock Company, became the clock company for the elite of Germany and France. Her immediate ancestors emigrated from Berlin to the upper Midwest, and their German cousins included Marlene Dietrich, the notorious beauty and film siren of the 1930s, '40s, and '50s, whose mother, Josephine Felsing, was a cousin of my mom's dad, Paul. The Felsing women were stunning, according to Marlene Dietrich, something I can easily believe, considering the curves and cheekbones of my seven sisters in their youth and the continued generational proliferation of beautiful women in my family to this very day. Mom's sister Margaret, whom I first saw sitting at the kitchen table one morning when I was five, was so beautiful I nearly fainted at the sight of her: raven black hair, dancing jet-black eyes, flawless skin, perfect white teeth, stunning lips, a bell-like laugh and yes, stacked to boot. It's really ridiculous, honestly.

Grandpa Paul Felsing was typically German: taciturn, dry sense of humor, wavy hair combed back. I loved him, and so did everyone else. Grandma (Mary) Felsing was of the Leonard clan, a large Scotch-Irish family boasting nine children. Up the road lived her childless aunt and uncle, of whom she was very fond; so fond, in fact, that her own parents let her and her sister go live with them permanently, giving them the children they always wanted, and solving the crowding problem in their own home at the same time.

Mom, born in 1935, was the eldest of six – three boys and three girls. She looked almost exactly like her sister, Helen, who was just a year younger, if that; and then there was Arthur, who had Von Recklinghausen's Disease and had to have a brain tumor removed at two, leaving him blind in one eye; and then David, a hilarious, handsome, and ornery fellow just like Grandpa; then Margaret; and then Mac, a straggler born to Grandma when she was forty. That was the clan. They lived on the farm in northwest Iowa where Grandpa minded his fields and animals and played pranks on the neighbors while Grandma took care of the kids with an iron discipline, tended her rock gardens and goldfish ponds, and ruled as the family matriarch.

Life on the farm near Laurens was typically pretty calm and routine. The most exciting thing to happen was the appearance one day during World War II of a Japanese bomb descending into Grandpa's field by parachute, having been launched God-knows-where and ending up uselessly unexploded on his northwest Iowa farm. That aside, things were generally so calm that Grandpa had to make his own excitement by taunting the neighboring farmers with periodic pranks, such as propping up a dead frozen skunk in the neighbors' barnyard, eliciting an early morning volley of gunshots followed by a pickup door slamming, a screen door opening, and an aggravated buddy yelling at Grandpa, as he sat having his morning coffee: "God-damn you Paul Felsing! You're gonna get it!" And sure enough, eventually he did.

Mom was a typical oldest child – responsible, dignified, respectful, and an overachiever. She was the valedictorian of her class, and destined for great things, even in the relatively female-oppressive 1950s. After graduation, she left for Des Moines where she studied at the American Institute of Business and worked downtown in admissions at Iowa Methodist Medical Center. I have a picture of her from back then, leaning against a tree at the family farm: pretty, brunette, thick glasses from all that studying, great smile, and yes, also stacked. She was a picture of things to come, a generation of women who would chafe at being held back by men and eventually escape those iron shackles. She was just a bit too early, though, to escape.

Dad (John Cornelius Coster) was, well, I guess you would call him a hick, smart though he was. He was born in 1925 in a farmhouse on the Des Moines River bottom where Lake Red Rock sits today, just south of Pella, Iowa. His sister, Mary Belle, was born a couple years later. The two of them grew up there in relative obscurity, as there was no one around to speak of, just other farmers across the river and a few villages throughout the woods. They attended a one-room country school at Coal Port a couple miles away, pretty much trudging uphill in both directions to get there and back, come hell or high water. Grandpa (Cornelius John) Coster cut down trees and dropped them across the river so they could walk over them on their way to the schoolhouse rather than taking an old boat all the way across. I guess one day Mary Belle fell off and landed splat in the mud on the way to school, but so what. That was only one of the many misadventures of their rustic lives. No indoor plumbing, hard work every day in the fields and in the woods, sawing timber by hand, taking care of livestock, living through the periodic river floods that invaded the first floor of the house and washed protesting hogs down the river on rafts of logs, canning vegetables to get through the winter, washing clothes by hand – you know, the usual stuff. By the time Dad was seven he'd lived through a bout of polio and nearly died from appendicitis. His right side was permanently weakened and a little atrophic from the polio, and his right shoe was built up. In spite of that, he grew into a handsome fellow and managed to get through the twelfth grade, migrating to Knoxville to finish up at the high school there. He remained on the farm with Grandpa after graduation and served a stint in the service during the Korean War, but remained stateside due to his polio muscles, and didn't see any combat. At the time Mom met him he was nearly thirty years old, and spending his weekends racing around Des Moines with his revved-up Chevy, enjoying the roar of the glasspacks echoing amongst the downtown buildings while looking for girls. Apparently, he drove about a hundred miles per hour everyplace he went.

Grandpa Coster was, I guess, something else again. Born in 1876, he was forty-nine when my dad was born and had already lived an entire life. His family was from Amsterdam, Holland. His father had changed the spelling of the family name from the original "Koster" to "Coster," as he thought the new version looked more American. Great-grandpa Coster moved all the way to South Carolina from Knoxville, Iowa, when Grandpa was just a kid – it was his only solution to the problem of birth control – leaving his wife and family of five in Iowa to struggle alone with the money he sent back, figuring, I guess, it was better and safer to be apart than risk the life of his wife again with any more difficult births.

So, Grandpa basically grew up fatherless and did what any youngster would do under similar circumstances in the

1880s – he left home at age twelve, was arrested as a horse thief in Mason City at fourteen, and would have been hanged if it hadn't been for my great-grandmother rescuing him at the last minute. He spent his teenage years jumping trains and riding around the entire country, doing odd jobs, and gambling. He was a card shark. He was also eventually an inventor, a farmer, a businessman, and a sawmill owner, things that made him bigger than life. He was self-made and had a strong presence. Legend has it that in his twenties he was married to Nancy Mae Dalton, a sister of the notorious Dalton Brothers Gang which terrorized the countryside robbing banks and trains. Apparently, there was a child born – a son – but no one knows what happened to him, nor does anyone know much about Grandpa's connections to all these people and what sort of shenanigans he may have been up to before he ever met my grandmother.

Grandma Coster's family was from England. Her original name was Maude Blackman. The family patriarch, William Hallows Blackman, was born in 1796 and lived for nearly a hundred years. He migrated to the United States from Essex Co., England, in 1829, with his wife, Susan Holder, and six children, and eventually worked his way west into Iowa in 1859, following four of his now grown children, the descendants of whom landed in the Newton and Knoxville areas.

And how Maude Blackman met Cornelius Coster, I have no idea. But Grandpa was forty-eight and Grandma was a spinster at thirty-eight when they married, and it was an unusual combination, Grandma, with her dignified English bearing, and Grandpa, with his lawless and self-made ways and demeanor. They had a hard life on the farm on the Des Moines River bottom, with the big saw mill and tons of work to do, and they fought a lot, screaming at the tops of their lungs all the time. Grandma found little room for dignity, common courtesy, and finery in the pioneer world of my grandpa's making. Strong personalities can make for cantankerous marriages. They can also be passed down from generation to generation. So can intelligence and longevity. So, you begin to see what sort of man my father was bound to be as a result of this household of contradictions.

So, one day, Dad, on one of his trips to Des Moines, happened to stumble upon Mom at a dance at the Tromar Ballroom where she had gone with another girl from Laurens. She was eighteen, and he was twenty-nine and had been taking ballroom dancing lessons at the Arthur Murray Dance Studios. Dad was specifically there to find a wife, new dancing skills in hand, and for some reason, he was utterly smitten with Mom, and Mom allowed herself to be smited. She later told me she wasn't in love with him – how could she be – but upon the advice of her Grandma McNee she married him anyway. "He has everything one needs to be a good provider. You can learn to love him." Marrying a good provider was really important, as most women couldn't possibly expect to have a career, and it was a shame to be without a husband in the 1950s.

Dad took an apartment in Des Moines so he could properly court Mom, and after a three-month whirlwind romance they married in March, 1954, and moved into a trailer on one of Grandpa Coster's farms south of New Sharon. Grandpa had paid for that farm with cash he won playing poker during the Depression.

Right away, Dad began building Mom the house of her dreams, a big modern ranch with a kitchen full of Hotpoint appliances, including the unheard-of luxury of a dishwasher. The house was so fantastic for its time, it was featured the next year in the local paper, with a big front-page picture of Mom snapping peas at the kitchen table, her pregnant abdomen discretely hidden below the table top, her Hotpoint appliances grandly displayed in the background, and any dreams of a college education and career solidly put behind her.

They were a mismatch from the start. Different philosophies of life, different educational backgrounds, different goals, and different expectations and opinions about literally everything. Mom was gentle, smart, well-read, and funny. Dad had domineering traits and used sarcasm like a filet knife. Mom spent many nights in tears at Dad's insensitivity and callousness, and Dad didn't understand Mom's more refined ideas and desires, or why she'd fall apart at what he considered to be normal conversation at ninety decibels. In spite of everything, they occasionally had their tender and honest moments like most couples, and some really hilarious ones, and on the whole of it I guess Mom decided it was worth staying. Plus, she pretty much had to anyway.

The one thing they could for sure agree upon immediately was a desire for a large family, so it was nice when they started right off the bat with twins. However, on the farm, work had to be done, pregnant or not, and twins often didn't survive in 1955. After a vigorous bout of spring cleaning, Mom went into labor and delivered two boys, Neal and Paul. Within two weeks they were both dead, one of a kidney infection and the other with a lung infection. She and Dad were empty-handed after all of that, but they knew what to do; they did what everyone did when children died. They had another one. That's the way it worked.

The next year, Angela was born, Mom springing from bed with every tiny whimper, scared to death she'd lose this one too. Then came Mary Ann in 1957, Neal in 1958, me in 1960, Nancy in '61, Kathy in '63, Julie in '64, Sandy in '67, Ev in '70, Jonathan in '73, and Joey in '76. Thirteen babies in twenty-one years. How she managed this, I'll never know. A more exhausting pace of reproduction could hardly be imagined.

She had a thing about keeping each new pregnancy a secret, but we'd always guess anyway when we discovered her quietly knitting away on a new pair of baby booties. We calculated she was pregnant for nine years solid if you added them all together. And though she loved her little babies and loved being pregnant, she jokingly said she felt like The Old Woman Who Lived in a Shoe who had so many kids she didn't know what to do. And as we got older and wilder, she became particularly fond of the part of that nursery rhyme where the old woman "spanked them all soundly and sent them to bed."

It came to pass that Mom taught me how to sew, and knit, and sing, and take care of kitchen things in the house, in exchange for my companionship and never-ending supply of information about the wondrous world around us. She mined my interest in plants and animals as an aid for developing her rock gardens around the house. I had a never-ending supply of suggestions, of course. And I was an easy, happy little personality, not prone to fits or demanding much. By all reports I became Mom's favorite, or at least that's what I'm told today, and I can find no evidence to the contrary. Perhaps I was the substitute husband she really needed, though just a little boy. Not all the characters were yet born in 1964, but the family dynamic was already set, and the future of our family was upon us, though we couldn't see it that way, of course. Angela was already the most responsible as the eldest daughter, Mary Ann was already a sickly little imp, Neal was already rough and tumble and a Future Farmer of America and thus Dad's perfect favorite, Nancy and Kathy were just toddlers, Julie was a baby, and I was, well, different than the rest of them.

"You put him down, John Coster!" Mom hollered. "That was your own fault! I said, PUT HIM DOWN!"

The kitchen was upside down, my ankles in a painful vise-grip, my arms and head swinging violently and banging on the blue linoleum tiles. The air-intake of the fridge was moving crazily close to my eyes; I could see wisps of dust clinging to the metal edges. Chair legs and human legs were flashing about like a kaleidoscope. I was being beaten beyond belief, one powerful blow after another, into my back and butt, the air being knocked out of my lungs so fast I couldn't even get a breath to cry out. I struggled violently to get away, thrashing this way and that, twisting my back, grabbing wildly at the floor and fridge and chairs and legs whizzing by, unable to get any purchase on anything, struggling like an animal for its life – not thinking, only trying to get away at any cost.

There was one more powerful whack on my four-year-old behind and a quick tightening then loosening of the grip around my ankles as I was flipped wildly upright into the arms of my mother, landing in soft safety and away from the tyrant who'd just ruined everything in my world.

I could finally breathe, and I bawled and hollered until all I had left was that occasional unexpected gulp of air that comes when there's nothing left to bawl, gripping Mom like a baby monkey hanging on for dear life as she carried me to the living room and plunked herself down into her favorite rocker, furiously scolding Dad to beat hell the entire time. She was so angry she was weeping herself, rebuffing Dad's now ashamed efforts to smooth things over, jabbing him away with her elbow as he approached to lamely apologize, trying to rub my little head while I screamed in terror at his approach.

This scene all unfolded because of All-Star Wrestling and Dad's cruel streak, a streak that was, I'm certain, a result of his own rough childhood. As for the All-Star Wrestling, well, Dad was crazy about it for some reason. Though he scoffed at wasting money on entertainment and gifts and rarely allowed either one for Mom or us kids, he would sometimes violate his own principles and travel all the way to Des Moines just to waste money on real-life professional wrestling. He'd get so wound up watching it that one would think he was in the ring himself. The one time Neal and I went with him, I thought he was going to leap into the ring and attack the behemoth wrestlers – he scared me half to death. It was ridiculous. And if it happened to be on TV some night, he'd pace the living room and scream at the wrestlers, arms gesticulating wildly, leaping up and down out of his chair, laughing and booing and carrying on like nobody's business, convinced it was all real, every last dramatic leap and throw. If anyone suggested it was fake, he would get so mad he couldn't see straight. "It's not fake, you stupid idiot!" he would scream.

"Good grief, Johnny," Mom would sputter, watching him pace and holler at the TV like a lunatic, while she tried to nurse the baby. "Settle down before you have a heart attack!"

It could only be expected, then, that he would periodically demand spontaneous wrestling or boxing matches of me and Neal for his own entertainment, regardless of how important the book I was looking at, or the insect I happened to be carefully monitoring at the moment for some specific behavioral trait. He wanted us both to be at least amateur pro-wrestlers. He'd announce the match, demand the attendance of one and all, move the furniture back, put me in one corner, Neal in the other, and ring an imaginary bell to start the match. "In this corner, we have Neal Coster, the greatest wrestler in the universe, the meanest guy in America, the undisputed champion of the world!" he would sing out. "And in this corner, we have David Coster, the challenger, ready to beat him to a pulp!"

"Ding-a-ling-a-ling!" he'd holler from his referee position in one of the imaginary corners of the living room wrestling ring, "Time to wrestle!!!!"

Being the stouter but smaller of the two, I was actually the one who was usually beaten to a pulp by Neal, not the other way around, and I knew Neal was Dad's favorite son because he took him with him everyplace he went, and he really, in his heart, wanted Neal to win every time, not me. So, in some ways I hated this game, but occasionally Neal would do something that made me particularly angry, like twist my ears or poke me in the eye, and I would fly into a rage, develop superhuman strength, grab him, body toss him into the air, and slam him onto the couch, a sight that Dad lived for, and one that made him laugh and laugh. It was just like the real thing! Even though I hated wrestling, I felt very proud and happy whenever I made Dad laugh and brag about me. I really wanted him to like me as much as Neal, so I did what he wanted me to do and tried my best to do something dramatic and pummel Neal whenever we wrestled.

On this particular day, however, an atypical match was about to occur, and things didn't go as planned. Dad decided to play with me at lunchtime, having come in from his cultivating chores in the field. I was eating at the end of the table, with Dad sitting beside me in front of the refrigerator. Partway through lunch Dad playfully began punching me on the shoulder, so I punched him back. This was a game I knew. Every little bit, another punch from his big hand, then a tiny, furious punch from my little fist, like a gnat banging away at a moose.

"You're so weak," he teased. "Why don't you punch me as hard as you can? Come on! You pathetic little thing, punch me!" So, I made a face, and punched him quite a bit harder than usual in the arm. "That wasn't any punch! Geez, David, you're SOOO weak! Punch me like you mean it! Do it as HARD as you can, like a REAL wrestler!" he laughingly taunted. "Come on, punch me. Punch me! I want to see how tough you really are!"

By this time, I was tired of playing. My distaste for physical combat was stronger than my desire to make Dad happy by playing this game.

"I don't WANT to punch you anymore, Dad. I'm tired of this game now."

A frown flitted across his face. I could tell I had said the wrong thing.

"I said punch me." His voice changed, and now it was a command.

The game was over.

"No," I said. "I'm not punching you anymore. I don't like punching."

"Leave him alone and let him eat, Johnny," Mom said. "He's tired of all this punching, now stop it."

"You're not leaving the table until you punch me as hard as you can!" Dad yelled.

I didn't want to hit Dad as hard as I could. Why couldn't he understand that? I mulled my options and decided that I just better punch the hell out of him and get it over with. Maybe then he'd be happy again.

So, I gave in. I reared back with all my might and let him have it. My aim was on his shoulder, where I usually punched him, and I don't know what happened. Did he move a little? Did I move a little? But I punched him square in the eye so hard my knuckles popped. His head snapped back, his mouth gaped open, his eyes rolled back in his head, and he just sat there like that for a second. By the time he shut his mouth, shook the glaze out of his eyes and refocused on me, he already had a big black shiner around his left eye. I think I knocked him out for a second.

I was horrified. I sucked in my breath and stared. I knew I was dead. Rage took over his face. My heart stopped, my skin went cold, and the next thing I knew I was jerked out of my chair by my feet with such violence I didn't know what happened.

Mom clawed furiously at Dad, trying to save me, blocking his blows, grabbing at me and beating on him all at the same time.

"Johnny! Stop it! You monster! You got exactly what you deserved, you big lummox! Hand him over here before I give you another black eye, and I'm not kidding! Johnny! Give... him...HERE!"

She caught me as he flipped me back upright.

"What sort of monster are you?" she screamed. "What sort of terrible father would beat their son like that! You big stupid idiot! Someone needs to beat the daylights out of YOU!"

Dad started to holler that I deserved it, but Mom cut him off.

"Just shut up! Don't talk to me! There's nothing you can say to justify what you just did!"

Gulping for air, I looked up just long enough to see Dad glaring at me with his black eye, but it was long enough to see my destiny with him.

Dad had to answer a lot of questions from people in town about his black eye. For the next couple weeks when I was riding with him in the pickup, "learning how to be a farmer," he'd stop and tell the story at the store or gas station or mechanic's shop as if it were hilarious; how this tiny little boy of his had accidentally given him a black eye while playing a little boxing game. Imagine how strong the little tyke must be to have done such a thing! How funny it all was!

I went quietly along with it, smiling sheepishly like a good little boy, saying how sorry I was that the punch had hurt my dad, and embellishing the story to make people laugh. I wanted Dad to like me again and to know I didn't mean to hurt him.

His black eye healed in about three weeks. The beating was never mentioned again. But there were others: a whipping Neal and I endured after first being forced to strip naked and lie face down on the dining room floor, while my sisters were forced to watch the beating for added humiliation; an unexpected lambasting with a belt or open hand to drive home a point or to relieve a bad mood; and repeated whippings with wooden spoons, willow branches, yardsticks, and anything else handy that would lay a welt. Yet the emotional beating caused by his sarcasm and constant statements of how "worthless" we all were was even worse. Yet, it was the norm. Neal just shrugged it off, but not me. It was the price I would pay for being unusually emotionally connected and having an unusual memory for details. To this day I can see and hear, in my mind, every aspect of my father, every nuance of language and body; along with every reaction I ever had in response, from intense love to dread and hate. I learned to read Dad's mood and body language, and if there was the slightest hint of trouble when he came home at night, I'd promptly disappear or ease him into conversations that might lighten his frame of mind and save me. Most of the time, this worked, so I always searched diligently for the good, funny, happy dad that I knew was in there somewhere. But I saw every complicated bit of him as if he was made of glass, and I recognized his power over me and the danger of toying with him; his unpredictability meant he could easily destroy me, if even by accident. So, he was always the monster looming in the background, the one who might come home and happily toss me up to the ceiling and snuggle me and carry me around the house, or the one who might come home and beat me to smithereens. The terror was caused by the not knowing, by the mistake of greeting him with glee, only to be shoved aside or spanked for no apparent reason, and the sadness and longing from the mistake of lurking in the background too long to assess the situation, only to watch him happily sweep up a sister or my brother and smother them with hugs, instead of me – a missed opportunity. And thus, it went, on and on for all of us, the same but variable in each case, affecting us all differently, changing us and emotionally controlling us in ways we didn't comprehend until years later, when the chickens finally came home to roost.

Dad came in the front door, four-year-old Jonathan crying in his arms hysterically.

"What's going on?" Mom asked.

"This idiot kid was crawling around under the pews during the sermon at church, so I caught him and left. And now he's gonna get what he deserves," Dad said, through clenched teeth.

And with that, he walked into the living room, slammed Jonathan on the couch, rolled him over, and began waling on him. Mom told him to stop, but on and on he went, hitting him harder and harder for ten minutes straight.

"Now stay right there, you stupid kid," he said, as he got up to get something from the kitchen, leaving him sobbing face down in the cushion.

Five minutes later he was back for another round, spanking the boy violently for another ten minutes, although by now, Mom and the rest of us in the house were screaming at him to stop. Several of us tried to pull him off, but he wrested himself away and continued with the beating.

"Johnny, STOP IT! Crawling under the pews was not a big deal! Just STOP IT!" Mom yelled at him as he pushed her away.

He got up again and walked into the dining room, all of us yelling at him. Within five minutes, he was back at him again, spanking him with all his might. Jonathan, by now, had become silent from shock.

I walked up behind Dad and grabbed the V on the back of his overalls and yanked him off, knowing this was not going to end well for me or Jonathan. Dad spun and tried to push me away so he could get back at Jonathan, but I yanked him back again, hard. This time, he turned to face me, right fist pulled back. His eyes were black and malevolent, his face so enraged it was almost unrecognizable. He had never punched me in the face before, and at this point, I was in such a deadly rage

39

myself that I decided this was it, I was finally going to have it out with my dad.

"Just try it," I said, my own fist now pulled back. "It'll be the last thing you ever do."

His fist flinched a little, but then remained still above his shoulder, as he stared at me.

"Really?" I said. "You want to punch me out? Your own son? Go ahead, try it," I taunted.

His fist dropped to his side. He stared at me for a few seconds longer, then walked away toward the kitchen.

"You leave my brother alone, Dad, and I'm not kidding," I called after him, as he walked through the kitchen and laundry room, and out the back door.

MRS. CHASE

The first years of my life were just so pleasant, in spite of Dad. Long summer days playing in the cornfields and horse weeds, and making up games with Angela, Mary Ann, Neal, Nancy, and Kathy in the front yard. We padded barefoot through the layers of August dust on the farm lane to play with toy tractors and trucks in the dirt pile, walked on discarded oil barrels like circus performers across the front yard, played freeze tag, jumped off the machine shed roof on the rope swing – with Dad pushing us wildly and scaring us to death, climbed trees to see what was in the nests up there, and dammed the creek a mile from the house to make little swimming holes, catching minnows and crawdads to bring home in jars.

We caught lightning bugs and June bugs, put them on the girls, and watched them scream and run. I rode on the bulldozer seat with Dad, hanging on for dear life while he knocked down trees and moved dirt at his other farm on the river bottom. I caught mice in the basement, fed crickets to my pet toad – Little Big Eyes – who lived in the basement drain, shot sparrows with the BB gun, swung naked on the hemp ropes in the hay mow, and took flying leaps into the hay piles while Dad milked Blackie the cow.

Fresh kittens had to be played with, sweet corn had to be picked with Grandpa, canning had to be done with Grandma and Mom, peas had to be shelled and eaten in big gobs, straw-berries had to be picked, weeds had to be pulled, and all of Dad's interesting farm projects had to be inspected.

Cooped in the house for the winter, we roller-skated in the basement, knitted ridiculous scarves, made Christmas angels out of Reader's Digests, performed puppet shows and perfor-mance art, wrestled with Dad when he was in a good mood, played school with the old country-school desks in the base-ment Dad bought at auction, played "monster" in the base-ment, ate enormous piles of Mom's fried chicken, and told scary stories around the kitchen table, snorting hot chocolate out our noses, laughing and screaming. In the evening Mom, vivacious and fun, played the piano as we gathered around singing along to "Red River Valley" and "I'm a Lonely Lit-tle Petunia in an Onion Patch" and "Edelweiss" and a whole slew of folk songs. We got so good that our entire troop was invited to sing one Christmas for a big group in New Sharon, the crowd laughing hysterically as we sang "I'm Gettin' Nut-tin' for Christmas," looking for all intents and purposes like the Von Trapp Family Singers with our matching shirts and dresses and stairstep heights all in a row.

From April to October, I wore only a pair of shorts, my skin golden, my buzzed hair a halo of white, my bare feet tough as nails. I could run at full speed barefoot on the gravel driveway. Once a week I got a bath whether I needed it or not, usually with my brothers and sisters all at once, since so many of us could fit in our one bathtub. Mom toweled us off one by one as the old Iowa dirt went down the drain with the soapy water. Oh, my bed felt so good at the end of those long exhausting days! A quick kiss on the forehead from Mom and off to sleep I'd go, snuggled in the bottom bunk in the room I shared with Neal, thoughts of dead Aunt Cora long forgotten. The girls in the room next door giggled and called out until we each fell asleep one by one, Mom hollering down the hall every two minutes, "Be quiet and go to sleep!" Life seemed about perfect, even with a scary Dad.

But then I had to go to school. This should not have come as a surprise. I had plenty of warning. Everyone else ahead of me had gone.

But somehow, I was still shocked when I was told to put on some shoes, my new jeans, and the shirt Mom made for me, get my Crayolas and paper, and get in the car.

I didn't resist, but I couldn't have been more apprehensive. A short two-mile ride in the Cadillac (Dad always got one for Mom) and up the stairs into the biggest building I'd ever seen, and there I was, face to face with my unwanted future.

The Lacey schoolhouse was a small brick building in the smallest of towns, a town founded and named after a former Iowa state senator from just down the road in Oskaloosa. The school housed a few students in each class, from kindergarten to sixth grade. After that, the kids were all farmed off to New Sharon, five miles up the road, to go to the junior/senior high school, a future so distant I had no knowledge of it. All I knew at the moment was that I was in a strange room in a huge building with a lot of people I didn't know.

Well, actually, I guess there were only about fifteen of us, but it seemed like an awful lot of strangers to me, and I wanted no part of it.

The students all looked up expectantly when I entered the room, and Mrs. Chase leaped up from her desk to welcome me. She was beautiful and full of energy, and so happy! I loved her immediately, though I was afraid of the whole scene. Her hair was brunette and put up, her skin was flawless, and she wore those cat-eye glasses that were so popular in 1965. She must have been all of twenty-one. She gave me a big hug, told me how happy she was to see me, picked me up and plopped me down on her lap, grabbed a piece of paper, and asked me to draw some pictures for her while she talked to Mom for a minute. So, while she talked to Mom, I drew her some pictures of ducks and people and flying birds and water. She smelled good. I began to get happy and comfortable and thought this wouldn't be so bad after all, sitting on Mrs. Chase's lap and drawing pictures all day long.

Eventually, Mrs. Chase called out to the class. "This is David," she announced. I looked up sheepishly, wondering why those other unfortunate kids had to sit at desks, poor things.

So, there I sat on Mrs. Chase's lap, surveying my new landscape, when suddenly, I noticed Mom had vanished. I was momentarily stunned, but quickly regained my composure. Quick as a wink, I was off Mrs. Chase's lap, out the door, and taking the stairs two at a time. Those years of climbing trees, swinging in the barn, racing up and down the driveway, and wrestling my brother came in handy as my little body leapt to my command, muscles taut with each flying leap down the stairs, balancing like a cougar, spinning on the balls of my feet, dodging this way and that to escape the outstretched arm of Mrs. Chase, so aptly named at that moment.

I saw my mother's coat as it departed around the outside door, making me break out in a wail that could be heard for two miles. Mrs. Chase captured me at just that instant, her tiger-like instincts superior to mine, swept me up, and hauled me back into my prison, doing her best to calm me as I squirmed to escape. I was inconsolable for the next hour even though Mrs. Chase kept me at her desk, offering me suckers.

Over the ensuing days Mrs. Chase kept me sitting right beside her in my desk, daily moving it a little bit farther into the classroom to push me in with my classmates. She seemed to realize that I was like a child from some distant land, my life experience so far more like an African tribal child's than anything else. I was very poorly socialized and had really never met any kids except for my own brothers and sisters, never straying from the bubble of the farm, so this was more traumatic than one might expect of such a minor thing. I gradually overcame a little of my shyness and figured out how to play with the other kids at recess, write my name, tie my shoes, say the Pledge, and do all the things I had to do to get to first grade the next year. My relationship with Mrs. Chase was a special one, and I missed her when school was out the next May. Little did I know that she'd taken another job in a bigger school system and I wouldn't see her again until my high school graduation twelve years later, when she surprised us all by coming to check in with us, her special class, the very first one of her career.

The last time I ever saw her was at my wedding, when I was 21. She handed me a wedding gift. I opened the card. It read: "To my smartest, most interesting, creative, and favorite kindergartner." The gift was the framed drawing of ducks and water and flying birds I had made one day sixteen years before while sitting snugly on her lap at the Lacey schoolhouse. "I never had a kid like you ever again," she said, with a big smile.

"Here comes the bus!" I yelled at my little Adam. My god, he was so cute in his little jeans and his new shirt and belt, his

tiny backpack strapped snuggly on his back, his freshly cut blonde hair neat as a pin. He was jumping up and down with excitement. Two years of preschool and lots of homeschooling by his mom and lots of talking about the fun he was going to have had more than paid off. He wasn't even the slightest bit afraid! The bus pulled up, the doors were flung open, and he all but leaped onto the first step, though almost too high for his little legs. He was so little! Too little to be leaving me! I burst into tears as he turned to wave at me and Julie and his little brothers Seth and Sam, a big smile on his face.

"What are you crying about, David?" Julie asked as the doors slammed shut. "Yeah, Dad, what are you crying about?" four-year-old Seth said, now looking up at me for some reassurance that this was all okay, while one-and-a-half-year-old Sam hovered in Julie's arms, staring at me with his huge blue eyes.

"I don't know," I said, as I waved, and waved, and waved, swallowing my tears as the bus grew smaller and smaller on the horizon, finally vanishing in the dust.

POTS AND PANS

Most kids have really nice grandmothers, the types that frequently ask them to stay over so they can read, go to the zoo, bake cookies, play outside, and knit. At least, that was the impression I got from overhearing the conversations of my kindergarten classmates. What fun they had with their grandmothers!

Dad was thirty-five when I was born, and Grandma Coster was thirty-nine when Dad was born, so she was already old when I appeared on the scene, and she was tired and crabby. Dad had a picture of her as a beautiful, well-bred younger woman in a fantastic polka-dot dress and veiled hat, her English heritage obvious by her cheekbones and dignified posture. She looked exactly like Queen Elizabeth I. I'm not kidding – I've seen the tomb effigy of Queen Elizabeth I in London, and it looks exactly like me and exactly like my grandmother. It's eerie. The years on the river bottom slaving away as a pioneer woman in the early 1900s with my grandpa, who died of stomach cancer in 1956, had been hard on her though. Her hip was broken sometime in those years and it was never properly set, healing wrong and resulting in a very bad limp. She was unhappy, critical, and sarcastic most of the time, a very different person from the woman of her youth.

Since Grandpa Coster was long gone, Grandma spent six months of the year living with Dad and the other six months living with Dad's sister, Mary Belle. Thus, for the first eight years of my life, we nearly always had an old person living in the house, with mixed blessings. Grandma was pretty difficult. She wasted no time with niceties while tossing barbs about Mom's mothering techniques, cooking, house cleaning, and so on. Mom put up with it because she was too respectful not to and she knew Grandma didn't feel good most of the time.

Every morning, because she wouldn't allow anything different, Grandma made breakfast. I was subjected to a big glop of oatmeal and forced to eat it. I washed it down with a good dose of cod liver oil, Dad prying my resistant mouth open for this delightful treat. Some days I got eggs fried in an inch of Crisco instead, but usually, it was just the glop. It definitely needed salt.

Grandma's other job was washing the dishes. She'd turn this task to no one, and defended the sink as if it were her own battlefield, organizing a little army of dirty plates and dishes on the counter and attacking them with dish soap and a wire scrubber in a gigantic dishpan. She was the field marshal of her domain.

"Grandma, I need a drink of water," I said, out of breath from racing Neal up and down the driveway in my bare feet one morning.

She studiously ignored me.

"Grandma, I said I need a drink of water," I piped up again, a little louder this time.

"You can't have a drink right now, young man. I'm busy doing the dishes, can't you see anything? You'll have to come back later."

"But I'm dying of thirst, Grandma, I need a..."

There was a loud "BONG" as she whipped around and whacked me on the top of the head with a big pan. "I said NOT NOW!" she shrieked. "Get out of the kitchen!"

"MOM!" I screamed. "Grandma hit me on the head with a pan! And she won't let me have a drink of water! Come here and spank her, Mom!"

Mom put down whatever baby it was she happened to have at the time and tromped into the kitchen. "For heaven's sake, Maude, you don't need to hit him on the head just because he needs a drink! Here, David, I'll get you one." She pushed Grandma aside and got me a glass of cold water. I gulped it down, glaring murderously at my attacker.

"These kids shouldn't be allowed in the kitchen when I'm trying to do these damn dishes!" Grandma bitched. "How am I supposed to get anything done with these constant interferences?"

All I heard after that was "blah, blah, blah." I went back outside to find Neal and do something fun, rubbing my head. "Stupid Grandma; I wonder how she'd like it if I snuck up and banged her on the head with a pan, the shit-ass." I spit on the ground.

On another day that summer Angela and Mary Ann were playing with a couple of baby sparrows I had gotten for them out of a nest. They were still in pin feathers, quite ugly, but sort of cute at the same time. I was collecting bugs so the girls could feed the little things. It was funny to watch them gobble up whatever we poked into their gawping, rubbery beaks.

Grandma poked her head out the screen door, pan and dish towel in hand: "What are you silly girls doing with those baby birds? If you don't put them back in the nest, I'm going to chop their stupid heads off!"

The girls screamed. Angela ran in the house and told Mom while Mary Ann guarded the birds in case Grandma showed up with a knife. I heard Mom tell Grandma to stop scaring the girls as I flipped over rocks to find bugs for the birds.

About then a car drove in. This was such an unusual event in our daily routine that we all leaped up to see who it was, running around the car to find Helen Whitis, our wonderfully nutty neighbor lady. She'd brought something over for Mom but took a few minutes to tell us some jokes while we intently watched her great, ruby-red lips leaking lipstick onto her cigarette as she yapped boisterously away, smoke blasting from her nostrils and the depths of her cavernous throat. I was afraid of this beast of a woman, perpetually shocked by her audacity, her gravelly loud voice, and general unladylike behavior, yet intensely interested in her, so different from my mother! After a bit, she flipped a curl off her glasses with her cigarette and asked us to lead her to Mom, so the girls ran ahead while she straightened her tight skirt over her ample behind and primped her beehive hairdo, eventually clomping toward the front door in her high heels while I followed at a safe distance behind.

Suddenly, there was a shriek of horror from the front porch, followed by another. I looked up to see Grandma silhouetted in the door, paring knife in hand, and my screaming sisters holding up two headless birds while Helen, parked on one square high heel with cigarette in outstretched hand, muttered, "Well I'll be gawd-damned…"

And thus, it went. No wonder people wanted to come over just to see what was going to happen next at "The Coster Place."

Grandma would let out war whoops and blood-curdling shrieks that could be heard for three miles every time she imagined something was about to happen to one of us kids, playing innocently in the front yard. She scared Mom out of her wits. "Good grief, Maude, do you have to scream so loud? You scared me to death!" Mom would chide.

"Well, I thought one of those kids was going to get run over! There's a car coming down the road!"

"Maude, the kids are thirty yards from the road, that car is a half mile away, and it's the only one to come by so far today. For heaven's sake! Would you just stop your screaming all the time?"

At that, Grandma would burst into tears, declare she was unwanted, and limp stormily back to her bedroom to sulk.

In the evening, she brushed her waist-length silver hair, which she normally kept in a braid coiled at the back of her head. Afterwards she came to the living room, sat on the couch, and applied skin lotion. If I happened to walk by too closely as she attended to her beauty treatment, a cane would suddenly snake out, hook me by the leg, and drag me to her side. "Rub my feet!" she'd say. "And here, put this lotion on them." I always tried to wriggle free, but she had one hell of a strong grip for an old woman.

"I don't want to rub your feet, Grandma!" I squeaked.

"I don't care! Do it anyway!" she snapped. "And be quick about it."

I rubbed her feet for a couple minutes, studying her gnarled toenails, wishing my hands were someplace else. For once she was quiet.

"What do you want to do, David, ring the bell or climb the rod?"

"Neither one, Grandma. I know this joke. It's a bad one."

"No, it isn't. I changed the ending."

"You did not, Grandma. You've tricked me before. I'm not answering."

"No, no, really, I changed the ending. Just try it and see, now come on. What do you want to do, ring the bell or climb the rod?"

"Oh, for heaven's sake, Grandma, I guess I'll ring the bell."

"GO TO HELL!" she shrieked, laughing. "Tricked you! Ha-ha!"

I pouted. "That's not nice, Grandma. I changed my mind. I don't want to ring the bell. I want to climb the rod."

"Then go to God," she replied, a satisfied smile on her face.

By this time, Mom's parents, Grandma and Grandpa Felsing, lived on a big tract of timber along the Des Moines River, just below Red Rock Dam near Pella. Grandpa had retired from farming near Laurens, and spent his time combing the lakeshore for driftwood out of which he made fantastic lamps, canes, coffee tables, and knick-knacks. Their place was a fantasy land – a virgin timber (owned by Dad) on a bluff overlooking the river, full of wildlife.

I was crazy about animals and plants, so going there was my favorite thing in the world to do. I'd be out of the car almost before it stopped, into the woods, eventually finding my way down to the riverbank where I'd catch soft-shelled turtles, collect turtle eggs, find clams, catch little fish, and watch for birds. Grandma and Grandpa had befriended Gladys Black, the state ornithologist, and they all spent a good deal of time birdwatching, banding birds, and studying and writing reports about the birdlife around the lake.

In late April, we always went there to hunt for morels, often bringing home great bags of them to be fried in butter and flour, eating as many as possible before they suddenly vanished from the timber as quickly as they came.

If it were possible, I would have lived at Grandma Felsing's house.

The Felsings were neat, fun, sensible, well-spoken, and occasionally boisterous. The Coster family was noisy, impractical, impetuous, and chaotic. As a result, we rarely visited the Felsings, and when we did, Grandma usually made us stay outside and play so we wouldn't mess up her all-too-interesting house. She made dolls and wedding cakes, and had collections of beautiful things that we simply couldn't resist. She lived in terror of our visits. At first, it was just Mom and Dad and a few kids, but then five, six, seven, eight, nine, and eventually ten. It was just too much. We were lucky to get chocolate chip cookies on the outdoor steps!

So, one Grandma beat me with pans and hooked me with canes and screamed bloody murder all the time. The other was loving and interested but understandably distant; I was much older before I truly developed a relationship with them. It didn't matter much to me one way or the other. Somehow their lives had made them who they were, and that's just the way it was. It was all normal to me. This was what I had to work with.

"David, I'm taking Grandma Coster to Oklahoma to see a doctor. Do you want to ride along?" Dad asked.

"Where's Oklahoma? What's wrong with Grandma?"

"It's a long ways, probably at least twelve hours of driving. Grandma has stomach cancer, and there's a doctor there who thinks he can cure her. We'll take the van. Any of you kids that want to go can come along, but you'll have to sleep on the floor or on one of the seats in the van. Your mom's staying here to look after the babies. Getting you out of her hair for a while would be a good thing. We're just going to go and then turn around and come right back."

I wasn't so sure about this plan, but since most of the other kids were excited about going, I decided to go along. It was the summer of '68, and I was about to turn eight.

Along the way, Grandma intermittently peed in a bed pan, and Dad stopped just long enough to throw it out in the ditch. We stopped for gas a few times, but otherwise just stayed in the van. I watched the countryside go by, then slept on the floor of the van for a good long while. Late in the afternoon we arrived at our destination, a little building seemingly in the middle of nowhere. The dirt was such a bright red! I leaped out of the van to look for lizards, as I'd heard they might live way down here. There were ghostly locust trees with huge black thorns all over the place. I saw a few lizards, which I hunted while Grandma was seeing the doctor, but they were too quick for me. After fifteen minutes had passed, Dad escorted Grandma Coster back to the van and commanded us all to get back in, we were going back home.

"What happened?" I asked.

"Nothing. The doctor gave us some pills to try. Maybe it will work, but it's doubtful."

"Can we go someplace else, then, like to a lake or something?" I asked.

"Nope. We're heading home. Get back in the van. I think that guy's a witch doctor."

I don't know what time we got home, but it was dark and miserable sleeping on the hard floor of the van all those hours. Within two weeks I was ushered into Grandma's hospital room to bid her farewell. She had shrunk. Her tongue was dry and looked purple, and she could barely talk. Dad shoved me forward.

"Tell her goodbye, David," Dad said.

I didn't like this scene at all. "Goodbye, Grandma," I said in a whisper.

She touched my face with her withered hand, and made an attempt at a little smile. The next time I saw her, she was in a casket.

ABANDONED

Mom didn't know she'd abandoned us, and neither did Neal. I was the only one who knew, but it should have been obvious to anyone. She dropped us off to play at the park in New Sharon while she picked up some things at the store. Within fifteen minutes, I was done playing, as the park was as small as a postage stamp and had only a slide, some swings, and a little merry-go-round, and now she was nowhere to be seen. Where was she? And just then I saw her, speeding out of town in the Cadillac, going the wrong direction. I burst into tears. Neal tried to console me, but he hadn't seen her speed by, so was convinced I was mistaken. I resolved to walk home. I knew the way. Neal would simply have to come along. He held me back as long as he could, but there was no stopping me.

So, we took off, trudging south through downtown New Sharon, our six- and seven-year-old legs carrying us past Hinmon's Drugstore and Soda Fountain, M&L's clothing store, the café, and the tavern already reeking with smoke; on past the residential areas, past the Dairy Creme, and eventually to the cemetery on the edge of town. The twins were buried there, but I didn't know it. I kept looking for Mom, but she was nowhere to be seen. I'd definitely been abandoned. My path was set. Neal begged me to go back to the park, but I'd walked a good half mile and wasn't turning back. Neal threatened to go back without me, but I knew he wouldn't dare. We headed out of town on Highway 63 toward home, just another four and a half miles away.

Cars whizzed by, horns honking at us two tiny kids. I began to get embarrassed, feeling exposed on the shoulder of the road with the cars roaring by, so we took to the ditch where we could sort of disappear. We paused near a storm sewer grate; I looked down only to see that Neal was standing on a pile of huge bull snakes. It was May, and they were in a mating ball, looking for all intents and purposes like rattlesnakes. They vibrated the tips of their tails menacingly. They didn't like being stood upon one bit and writhed about under his shoes. He leaped off the pile with a "yow!" and the snakes raced into the storm sewer. Now, I was spooked. A pile of big snakes could only be a bad omen. I had to get home.

The problem was that people kept noticing us and honking, drawing a lot of attention. Up ahead I saw Mrs. Harkema's house. I thought if I could just get past there without being seen by anyone we knew, I could safely make it all the way home without being bothered. I told Neal to lay low and sneak through the ditch beside her house so she wouldn't see us, but she saw us anyway. There she was, standing on the edge of the lawn looking down on us. "What in the world are you boys doing?" I started to cry. "Mom left us in the park! I saw her drive out of town the wrong way, and disappear! I don't know where she went, but she's gone!"

Mrs. Harkema bit her lower lip. "I don't see how that could be," she said. "Eleanor wouldn't go off and abandon you in the park."

"But she did!" I cried.

Mrs. Harkema was baffled. Two small boys in a ditch a

mile from town, supposedly abandoned by their mother. It was the craziest thing she'd ever heard. "I'm taking you home," she declared. "Come with me, and get in the car." So, we got in the car and she took us home. I felt very embarrassed and was increasingly afraid that I had made an error in judgment; maybe that wasn't Mom who drove by, maybe it was just an identical car with a nearly identical mother in it. I hoped and hoped Mom would already be home, waiting for her long-lost sons to appear, devastated that her mind had slipped and she'd forgotten something important in town: her own sons. I imagined the joy of our reunion, the relief on her face at the sight of me, the only person that mattered in her life.

She wasn't home, of course. My reunion fantasy was replaced with an "oh, shit" instead.

Meanwhile, back in New Sharon, Mom was frantically driving all over town trying to find the two boys she'd told to stay in the park. Her shopping had taken about ten minutes longer than expected. That wasn't long enough for them to completely vanish off the planet, but vanish they had. Should she call the police? Did they go to someone's house? Had they been kidnapped? She cried as she raced around town, and then wondered if we'd somehow maybe gotten home. So, without further ado, she headed home at top speed, only to find us in the front yard, Neal reading the Sunday funnies, and me standing nervously beside him worrying myself to death.

She flew up the driveway in a cloud of dust, like Almira Gulch on her bike in Kansas before she turned into the witch, and leapt out of the car, her face red and tear-stained. She was so relieved to see us, and yet so mad, she didn't know whether to spank us or hug us, so she did both at the same time, carrying on like a lunatic while she dragged us to the house. I was sorry and embarrassed for all the excitement and upset I had caused, but didn't really understand what Mom was so wound up about. After all, I knew the way home. Needless to say, we were grounded and confined to our room except for meals for the rest of the day.

Two years later, little eight-year-old Pamela Powers was kidnapped from the YWCA in Des Moines by a man no one saw. Her parents had just left her for a few minutes. She was murdered, of course, and the story and newspaper headlines were sensational. Things like that just didn't happen in Iowa. I was horrified by the details of the story. "Now, do you see why I was so mad at you?" Mom seethed, grabbing me in a bear hug. She was, after two years, still both mad and relieved about our little incident.

All I could say was "yes."

HOW DO YOU SPELL "IT"?

I was the last person in my kindergarten class to learn how to tie my shoes. Everyone else had a nice little pair of cut-out paper shoes taped to the wall over the chalkboard for months, a sign of their success, with their name in Crayola brightly splayed across the toes, before my little pair of shoes finally showed up just before the end of the school year. It was one of my biggest embarrassments. Somehow my brain just couldn't visualize the physical concept of knot tying. But Mrs. Chase never gave up on me!

There were many others who never gave up either: Mrs. Patterson in first grade, Mrs. Moore in second grade, Mrs. Reece in third grade, Mrs. Seaverns in fourth grade, Mrs. Likens in fifth grade, Mrs. DeHoedt in sixth grade, and a multitude of others in junior high and high school. We were lucky to have some really dedicated teachers in our school system. They had different approaches, mind you, some more nurturing, others more direct.

"David! What are you doing back there? Am I going to have to move you to the front of the class?"

My first-grade cloud-gazing reverie was suddenly broken by the grating voice of Mrs. Patterson, startling me into dropping my pencil and nearly breaking my neck as my attention snapped away from the window and back to the front of the classroom.

"What? Nothing, I'm not doing anything," I mumbled.

"What? I can't hear you, David! I asked you what you're doing back there! Now answer me! The rest of the students are waiting! You're holding up the entire class!" She glared at me with her good eye, the other being smothered by an excessively baggy upper eyelid magnified through her powerful cat-eye glasses.

"Are you paying ANY attention at all to what is going on up here? ARE YOU?"

I was too frightened to respond.

"Well, we'll just see about that! Do you even know what word we're working on, David? Do you? Do you have even the SLIGHTEST idea?"

"It," I whispered.

"WHAT?" she screamed.

"I said, IT," a little louder now and with a trace of sarcasm appearing in my voice.

"Well, Mr. Smarty-Pants, if you were listening so well, perhaps you would like to tell the entire class how to spell 'it.' Do you think you can do that? DO YOU?"

"No," I whispered. "I don't know how to spell 'it.'"

"Well maybe you had better pay attention from now on instead of looking at the clouds outside, do you suppose? 'IT' is 'I' and 'T.' Two simple letters! The 'I' is short. So, now do you want to tell the whole class how to spell 'IT'?"

"I, T," I whispered.

"Louder!"

"I, T," I replied, my voice quavering.

"Okay then! Can we move on now? Everyone else is ready

to move on to three-letter words, the first of which is 'the.' Do you think you can pay attention for three-letter words?"

"Yes, Mrs. Patterson."

"Good! Now, three-letter words are really quite simple..."

The smallest things matter. Mrs. Patterson saved me. So did Mrs. Chase and the rest of them. Little by little, step by step they helped me do things that seemed too hard, and by fourth grade I became the spelling bee champion.

⤶

"What is this, Adam?" I asked, looking over my son's first-grade writing sample. "None of these words are spelled properly." Julie looked over my shoulder. "That's weird. He's too smart to be misspelling words. Look, the teacher gave him an A on it! What is going on?"

At the conference we requested the next day, Adam's teacher patiently explained that the school district had decided to implement a new program of spelling phonetically; "The kids," she explained, "will not be penalized for misspelling words. They will be simply writing them out the way they sound and can later learn how to spell them properly."

"That's a bunch of nonsense," I said. "Whose dumb idea was this? Anyone can see that the parents of all these kids are going to have to re-teach them everything about proper spelling when they get home each day!"

"It's a new system the school has decided to implement in order to make writing more enjoyable," the teacher replied. "We think in the long run it will improve performance."

"Enjoyable? Have you all completely lost your minds? We'll be undoing this damage for years to come! Who can we talk to about this? The Superintendent? The School Board? Whom?"

"I'm afraid the decision has been made and will not be un-

done. We are studying these children to see how they do with this new system."

"Well, we can tell you exactly how they will do! Badly!"

And they would have, if we hadn't formulated a plan to re-teach all the spelling words every single day.

MIND YOUR MOTHER ——————

"I'm going to town, boys. Do NOT go up on the hoghouse roof! And I MEAN it! If I get home and find you've been up there again, you're gonna get it!"

"Hmmm," I thought. "Getting up on the hoghouse roof sounds like fun; I guess I will!"

It hadn't occurred to me yet to get up there on this particular morning, but now that Mom had put the idea in my head, I could hardly wait for her to leave so I could do it!

As soon as the van was past the corner, I grabbed Neal and we ran out to the old hoghouse, a huge, unused, dilapidated building with an expansive flat wooden roof upon which we could see all the way to Oskaloosa. There hadn't been any hogs in it for years, Dad's first hoghouse having burned down, and a dip in the market later ruining the profit margin for raising hogs. It was fun up there, especially on warm summer days with the wind whipping through our buzzed hair. We'd bring our little cars and other playthings along, climb the interior posts to the roof edge, and swing our little bodies up through a couple of holes to arrive at this pleasant destination.

So up we went. We played hard for about twenty minutes, being mindful of the time as we expected Mom's trip to town to be very short. When we began to worry that we might be caught by her eagle eyes as she came down the road, we decided it was time to get down.

Neal went first, grabbing the edge of the hole in the roof and swinging like a monkey to an angled crossarm from which he catapulted to a perfect upright landing on the cement eight feet below. It was a new maneuver I'd never seen before.

"Wow, that was neat," I said. "I want to try that." But being small and only seven, I was scared. Sometimes I was still a little clumsy, and it was a long way to the floor.

With some coaxing from below I finally leaned in, grabbed the edge of the hole, and swung with all my might to the crossarm. "Yeah, just like that!" Neal cheered from the floor.

"Oh, shit!" I thought, though not saying a word as I grabbed frantically for the crossarm, well out of my reach. I swung back on one arm the way I had come, feeling my little hand losing its grip on the edge of the roof, and then a startled "thrill" in the pit of my stomach as I began to fall. The post, roof, crossarm, cement, and blue sky went by like a crazy quilt as I flew end-over-end to the floor. Then "CRACK," I heard the most awful clunk of bone on cement, followed by an instantaneous pain shooting around my skull into the backs of my eyes. I could see nothing but black with a kaleidoscope of pinpoint-colored flashes.

I shrieked, and shrieked, and shrieked, grabbing the back of my head, rubbing it violently, trying to rub out the intense pain. I felt Neal grabbing at me, pulling on me, trying to get me up, but I couldn't see him. I screamed and rubbed my head.

"Stop screaming!" Neal commanded. "Stop it! Get up and be quiet!"

He jerked me to my feet. I screamed again. The little flashes of light became bigger, turning into a collage of wood and cement and sky, then an actual picture. I shook my head back and forth like a dog shaking off water and screamed again. I leaned against the post, breathing fast and hard, trying to regain my bearings. I had landed flat on my back, just missing a two-foot length of re-rod poking straight up through the cement that could well have gone in the back of my head and out the front if I'd landed a few inches over.

Even without re-rod in my brain, I was in a bad way. I kept screaming. That's all I could do. The pain was throbbing intensely in the back of my head, the sunlight blinding me.

"Shut up!" Neal hollered. "Shut UP! You have to stop screaming!"

Neal thought I'd been mortally wounded, based on the "crack" of my skull on the cement, and could only think of getting me to the house. He grabbed my hands and pulled me, stumbling, out of the hoghouse and up the drive all the way to the house, quite a distance. I protested this rough treatment, pulling away to rub my skull, howling like a banshee. "Be quiet!" Neal said. "You HAVE to stop bawling! Mom's going to be home any second and she'll know we were on the roof! We're going to get it if she finds out!" I forced myself to tone it down to a whimper as we came in the back door, still rubbing my head.

I threw myself down on the couch in the living room. I couldn't see straight and my head throbbed. I felt sick and feverish. And then I heard the van coming in the driveway, and Mom waltzing in the back door with the groceries. I made myself be really quiet, grabbed a blanket, and rolled over, face to the back of the couch.

"What are you doing on the couch, David?"

"Oh, just resting. I feel a little sick for some reason."

"Hmmm," Mom said. She came and rolled me over, looked at my face, felt my forehead for a fever, looked for rashes, and snuggled me back in. "You do feel a little hot. Why don't you just rest? I'll get you some aspirin." So, I took the aspirin and laid there. I was way sicker than I looked, and I knew it. But there was no way I was going to tell Mom I had fallen off the hoghouse. No way. I was more scared of what she'd do to me when she found out than I was of my bashed-in head. I kept feeling the back of my scalp to see if there were any dents indicating a skull fracture, but I couldn't find any, so figured I was probably okay.

So, I lay there all day, getting sicker and sicker. I threw up. I couldn't sit up without getting dizzy. Mom puzzled over me, reexamining me, asking me questions about this and that, trying to figure it out. She'd never seen anything like it. Aspirin, cold cloths to my forehead, chicken soup, nothing seemed to help. She eventually got worried enough to move the couch over by the kitchen door so she could watch me while she made supper, and wondered out loud if she should take me to the hospital, remembering Mary Ann's nearly fatal bout of meningitis a few years earlier. "NO! I hollered. I'll be fine! Don't take me anywhere."

The summer went on, and I didn't die.

In 1983, I went back home from medical school in Oklahoma for a visit. Mom was talking about various things that happened when we were growing up, some of which were near fatal, when I piped up and said, "Remember that time I was so sick for three days and you couldn't figure out what was wrong with me?"

"Yes," she replied. "That was the strangest thing."

"No, it wasn't," I said. "I fell off the hoghouse roof and landed on the cement. My head just barely missed the steel re-rod

poking out of the cement." There was a dumbfounded pause.

"You did what? You could have died! Why didn't you tell me?"

"Well," I said, "I thought I'd get a spanking, so I'd better not tell. Now you can't spank me, so I'm telling you."

Mom remained flabbergasted, staring at me for a moment. How in the world could I possibly think she'd spank me when I was laying there with a head injury? I should have seen a doctor! I should have been in the hospital!

"I lived," I said, "And my brain still works okay."

"You were lucky," she retorted. "I can't believe you didn't tell me."

There was a pause as she processed this information.

"By the way, young man, what else haven't you told me that I should know?!"

I grinned. "Lots!"

KILL BILL ────────────

We had lots of animals on the farm; some were pets, others were for human consumption or produced things we needed. One of our favorite things was to go with Dad to the barn to milk our cow, Blackie. She was a big black-and-white Holstein, nice as pie. She stood quietly while Dad skillfully coaxed her milk into a big stainless-steel pail, occasionally shooting a stream into the mouth of his favorite yellow tom-cat, who sat lurking in the corner. Dad frequently let us try our hand at milking as well, but our little fingers were not adept at the practice, so it was encouraged more for Dad's amusement than anything else. We'd otherwise feed Blackie handfuls of hay, and scratch her head, and rub her smooth coat while Dad milked. She was very patient with our little hands traversing her various hills and valleys.

We loved Blackie and couldn't imagine life without her. Every evening we walked with Dad across the field to the breezeway where he'd pour the milk into the separator and we'd gleefully watch the various spigots spewing forth the cream and milk in separate containers. We dipped our fingers into the cream enough times to get our hands slapped. There was nothing so tasty!

When I was about eight, Blackie stopped giving milk. She was very old by then. When animals get old on a farm there is only one thing that happens: death, one way or another. I wasn't yet old enough to have that concept firmly established in my head, Aunt Cora notwithstanding, so when Dad announced he was selling Blackie, I was stunned; how could he sell our pet?

The answer was obvious of course. Blackie was not a pet; she was a milk-cow. We only imagined she was a pet. In short order Dad explained the difference, with the primary point being that HE determined which farm animals were pets, and Blackie didn't fit the farmer's definition of a pet. Well, okay we thought. Maybe we could go and visit her at her new home.

"Is Dub buying her?" (Dub was our farmhand and neighbor.) "Yeah, Dub's buying her. He'll be takin' her to the locker for meat."

We all looked at Dad with puzzled expressions.

"What's a locker?"

"Well, it's a place where cows and pigs are turned into meat so people can have something to eat," Dad replied. We stared at him with a slowly growing awareness and then all at once began screaming at him. "You murderer! You can't kill Blackie! We're going to save her! We'll take her away and hide her. How could you do such a thing? She's our pet! Leave her alone!" Dad merely set his jaw and told us all to shut up and go to bed, the decision had been made and that was that. He wouldn't listen to another peep out of us and we were not to shed another tear. End of story. It was just like *Charlotte's Web*, but didn't end so well.

So, Blackie went to the locker, and Dub and his family ate her. We were really mad about it and turned up our noses at every invitation for hamburgers or steaks at Dub's house even though we adored him and loved hanging out with his kids, Benny, Tony, Rex, and Rocky. We just couldn't believe they were eating Blackie.

◈

It's twenty-six years later; I'm in the kitchen with Julie discussing how we are going to tell Adam, Seth, and Sam that their pet bottle calf, who is now a great big steer named Bill, has to go to the locker.

Bill was a gift from the boys' Grandpa Augustine (Julie's dad), who thought that no kid should be bereft of the experience of raising a little calf by hand on a bottle. Bill was just a little runt (literally) that had been birthed unexpectedly in the feedlot, and something had to be done with him anyway, so the boys raised him with a lot of help from Julie and me. Bill proved to be a bit of a handful, but was pretty tame and pleasant to have around in the old shed out back on our acreage. But a year had passed now and he was finished growing. We weren't farmers, and it was time to put him in the freezer.

Julie was very worried about the boys' reaction to our announcement. We talked about the psychological impact of slaughtering their pet and then serving him up for dinner. How in the world can such a concept be made palatable to a trio of boys who are only six, five, and three? "Just tell them the truth," I said, early the next morning, as I got ready for work, remembering my own emotional reaction to the unexpected loss of my pet cow Blackie. "Every detail; they already know farm animals are raised and taken to the market; your dad has talked about it before. They eat pork and beef and chicken. They know animals are killed for meat. Just tell them it's time for Bill to go to the locker and be made into steak and hamburger. I think they'll be fine." And off to work I went.

Julie wasn't so sure, thinking about it for a few more hours

71

before finally announcing the plan that afternoon, as the boys sat at the table eating SpaghettiOs.

"Boys, I have something to tell you about Bill," she began.

"What?" they all asked at once.

"Well, you know how I've told you that someday we'd have to send Bill away when he got to be too big? Remember that? He's too big now. We can't take care of him anymore in that tiny pen. We have to send him away."

"Okay," the boys replied.

They continued to eat their SpaghettiOs, seemingly unalarmed by this bit of information. Julie paused for a moment, thinking about how to begin again. She finally just said it.

"We're going to have to turn him into meat for the freezer."

At this, the boys looked up from their bowls. "How do you do that?" Adam asked.

"Well," Julie replied, "first a man comes in a special truck made to haul cattle. But before he can put Bill on the truck, he has to kill him and drain his blood out." She winced when she announced this part. The boys merely looked at her.

"How do they kill him?" Seth wanted to know.

"They shoot him in the head," Julie replied. "In the old days, they cut their throats, but now they shoot them first to reduce any pain, and then cut their throats so all the blood can run out; otherwise, the meat is ruined. Then they take them to the locker where they are sliced up into different cuts of meat and hamburger. It's pretty awful, I know. I'm sorry I have to tell you this."

The boys looked at her for a few seconds.

"Can I shoot him too?" Adam asked, suddenly very interested in killing Bill.

"Yeah! I want to shoot him too," yelled Seth.

"Me too," mumbled three-year-old Sam between gulps of milk.

"Can I shoot him, Mom? I really want to shoot him!" yelped Adam gleefully. "Can I shoot him in the head?"

Julie was mortified. What sort of monsters had she been raising?

"What about the skin, Mom?" Seth asked. "Can I have Bill's skin to hang on the wall in my bedroom?"

"That would be really neat!" Adam screamed and giggled in delight.

"No! You can't have the skin and you can't shoot him, you little devils!" Julie was shocked. "Finish your lunch and go play! We'll talk more about this when your dad gets home!"

And so, it went. Every evening Julie called the boys away from their toys for dinner, a call that was studiously ignored until she sweetly sang out, "It's Bill!" Bill, it turned out, was absolutely delicious.

TEACHER'S PET ————————

One day, a teacher beat the tar and nicotine out of me. I was sauntering up to the school doors, as recess was about over, just minding my own business, when Jeff Crosby appeared by my side with a handful of pea gravel.

"Watch this!" he said, as he hurled the gravel with all his might, right through an open window into Mr. Van Arkel's classroom.

Now, I knew that whole Crosby clan to be ornerier than they should be, but nevertheless, I was unprepared for this abrupt shift in my day. I stood there, mouth agape, unable to respond to his display of unseemly behavior, or comprehend what could possibly have been going through his head to do such a thing. Well, about two seconds later, my mouth got a lot wider when gigantic Mr. Van Arkel barreled out the door, huge belly bouncing, angry darting eyes looking this way and that for the rock thrower, eyes that quickly homed in on me as I stood there all alone. He wrenched me off my feet by one arm and made me the recipient of one major beating. I had enough sense to scream bloody murder, startling Mr. Van Arkel out of beating me into shaking the teeth out of my head instead. I finally managed to scream in his face that I didn't do it – Jeff Crosby did. He dropped me and stormed around the corner where Jeff stood hiding, grabbed him by the ear, and dragged him into the schoolhouse.

He did not, however, beat him. Not even one little swat.

So, there I stood, bawling my head off, ashamed and humiliated, until two other teachers who witnessed the event hurried over to help me. Eventually, Mr. Van Arkel came back and sort of apologized, telling me the beating was really my own fault for just standing there. How was he supposed to know I hadn't done it?

There were a few other teachers my classmates and I had, on occasion, to shy away from. Even those of us with perfect grades and near-perfect behavior were not immune to the vagaries of being a student in the '60s and '70s. Corporal punishment for various offenses was still in vogue, and certain teachers were quite creative with its application.

"What are you doing over there, Maxine?" Mrs. Lynnville barked. "Get your book out like I told you to and quit your messing around!"

"I can't find it!" Maxine replied.

Poor Maxine. That was the wrong answer, I could tell easily from my secure perch at my desk across the room. I had been gauging Mrs. Lynnville's body language all morning. Her back was stiff, her arm movements like whiplashes as she smashed the chalk across the board, her tone deadly as she rammed verbs and adjectives down our throats. Her asthma was acting up; she'd been coughing goobers onto the chalkboard off and on all morning, furiously wiping them off with her sleeve as she continued her violent cursive. Her clothes were askew and her usually perfect beehive hairdo had dangerous wisps hovering about, like wall clouds around a tornado.

She glared at Maxine, one hand on her overly-generous hip, the other tightly gripping the chalk. "If your desk wasn't such a ridiculous mess, you might be able to find your stupid book once in a while, Maxine. Now quit rummaging around and find it! I've never seen such a hideous mess, you stupid girl."

Maxine was crying now, her last mistake, as she continued to dig through the papers and books in her over-stuffed desk, the lid up, the shameful mess apparent to all who dared look.

"Stop your bawling!" Lynnville barked again, this time, stomping over to Maxine's desk with her high-heeled shoes gouging the floor. "Apparently you need some help!" she snapped. And with that, she bent over, grabbed the desk by the corners, and turned it upside down in Maxine's lap, emptying the maze of contents all over her and the floor. "Now get down there and clean it all up! And find your work book in the process! I'd better not EVER find this sort of a mess in your desk again! You'll stay after school as long as it takes to straighten it up!"

By this time, Maxine was in hysterics and could only blubber around on the floor in the midst of her pile of stuff. Lynnville glared at her for a second longer, grabbed her by the collar, and hauled her out the door to the principal's office. The rest of us were frozen statues for the rest of the week, not daring to move or breathe in her class. We never knew when she might go off like a bomb.

Lynnville wasn't the only one who was potentially lethal. Mrs. Daniels kept a murderous eye on everyone as she walked around the classroom with her big ruler, whacking any kid across the back of the head or knuckles who dared look at her. Of course, for some of the boys it was a badge of honor to be whacked by the teacher and then hauled away to the principal's office; they kept a sort of ongoing tally with bragging rights going to those with the most whacks and trips.

Mrs. Smith had a particularly bad reputation for smacking us around. She was a substitute teacher, old as dirt, and about as wide as a truckload of it. Perpetually unhappy, she took her misfortunes out on the students in her classes, the smallest infractions resulting in pinches, smacks, detentions, trips to the office, and repeated whacks on the back of the head. We hated her. She was also a lousy teacher.

We were having a particularly bad day with her one spring morning. Multiple classmates had been punished and sent to the office. Mrs. Smith was in a foul mood. "Line up for lunch!" she hollered. "And be quiet! All of you!" We lined up in alphabetical order. We were starving, and exhausted from watching so many beatings that morning. She took the head of the line. "If I hear one peep out of any of you, there will be no recess! Do you understand me?" All was silent. "Good!"

On her orders, we marched to the stairs, whereupon turning to take a breath and berate us once more, Mrs. Smith fell from her precarious perch on the top step. Her eyes flew wide, her arms windmilled like mad, and then, over she went, bouncing down the stairs backward with muffled thuds and grunts, unceremoniously splatting on the landing below, knocking the swinging doors open with her huge ass before rolling to a final standstill. The doors, swinging back at their assailant, now lying groaning on her back, whacked her over and over in the head, beating her senseless.

TO PEE OR NOT TO PEE —————

As usual, Nancy was following us. We – Neal, his best friend from school, Ed, and I – looked furtively over our shoulders as we tripped along the dirt lane to the "tin" barn, as we called the enormous granary my grandfather built many years before.

"Throw a clod at her," Neal said. "Hurry!"

I bent over, collected two hard clods, turned, and chucked them at her with deadly aim, something I had practiced since I was a toddler. "Go away, we said!" I hollered at her. She deftly sidestepped, the clods striking uselessly in the dust. "No!" she screamed back. "I said I'm coming too! And you can't stop me!"

"Let's run," Neal said.

Neal and I had hideouts all over the farm, but our favorite was in the top of the granary. There we could build things with old boards, walk the rafters like acrobats, hide in the cupola and spy across the landscape for invaders, invent codes and languages and hide the keys so no one could find them, and so on. One of our favorite things to do in the summer was to strip naked and leap off the high beams into the piles of soybeans stored below. There is no need to explain it; it's just fun to fly naked through the air. The initial leap was frightening, as the drop was a good fifteen feet or more, but the adrenaline rush was great. Today, though, we had a friend over, so the clothes would stay on. We first got the idea of stripping when jumping after we got sick and tired of digging all the beans out of our shirts, and pants, and socks, and shoes, and underwear. At first, we did it because it was just easier to jump without clothes and avoid the task of cleaning all the beans out of them later, but as we got older, it became a thrilling, semi-erotic routine to run around naked, climbing the walls and leaping and rolling around like wild monkeys. We talked about boy things, about what sex must be like, since we were hearing talk at school. Of course, girls were not allowed in this boy-world. Whether or not we were fully clothed, we had to get rid of Nancy.

We ran as fast as our legs could carry us, swiftly leaving Nancy running and crying behind a wall of corn as we turned the corner and disappeared into the cool interior of the granary. "We have to make a quick getaway. She'll see us in a minute. Get to the ladder and go as fast as you can," Neal panted, as we leaped across the auger ditch and grabbed the bottom board of the wall ladder. Neal went first, followed by Ed, hand over hand, fast as gorillas, with me hot on their tails. By the time Nancy came bawling into the granary, we were carefully ensconced on a pair of boards laid across some beams twenty feet above her where we could spy on her as she wandered about looking for us.

"She better not try to come up here," Neal whispered.

"But what'll we do if she starts coming up the ladder?" I asked back in a whisper. "Our only escape is to go to the cupola and climb out on the roof, but from there we can't get off the barn. We'll be trapped!"

"I'll pee on her," Neal hissed.

"You better not! She'll see your dick! Plus, she'll tell Mom, and you'll be in big trouble! Forget it!"

Ed was snickering but was clearly uncomfortable with the idea of peeing on Nancy. "You probably better not do that," he whispered. "though it would be funny."

"I'm going to pee on her only if she tries to come up," Neal said firmly.

And then she started to come up.

Neal waited a moment to see if she'd really climb all the way up, Ed looking both amused and terrified the whole while. She kept coming, and when her little arms got to the fourth rung Neal finally stood up, unzipped, whipped it out, and peed with deadly accuracy, hitting her squarely on the crown of her little blond head.

Nancy, who'd been focusing on the great effort of climbing the ladder, suddenly put out a hand and said with a puzzled expression, "Hey, it's raining in here," to which I immediately guffawed, causing her to look up just in time to get hit in the face.

Needless to say, it didn't take long to figure out what was going on with warm pee splashing across her mug, nor did it take long for her to jump from the ladder and run to the house, bawling and screaming bloody murder – to tell Mom. The result was one of those rare moments when Mom felt it necessary to stop what she was doing and march herself to the barn to haul us out by the ears and give us a good going over. All but Ed, that is. His mom was called to pick him up, ruining what was supposed to have been his special day running around with Neal on the farm.

GODS AND DEMONS

Until the age of nine, I set foot in church on only a couple of occasions. I never thought about God. The concept of Bible school was totally alien to me, as was the idea of an invisible thing hanging around the universe spying on every move I made. But then Velma DeBoef stepped onto our front porch one sunny spring morning and changed all that.

I'll never forget the scene. An unknown automobile pulling up the drive, a knock at the door, and the appearance of a prim, smiling, middle-aged woman with a long braid rolled up on the back of her head, standing precisely where my grandmother had sliced the heads off those baby birds. I was immediately suspicious as we all gathered around the door to examine this stranger. She had a slight tremor as she smoothed her calf-length, nondescript skirt. She greeted us all with an artificially delighted "hello!" and immediately launched into an invitation to come to her church to "find the Lord," whoever and whatever THAT was. Mom came to the door and listened for a moment and politely told her we'd be happy to come someday if we ever decided we needed to. Velma was too smart to be put off that easily, of course. She kept showing up every Sunday afternoon, uninvited, and the next thing I knew, she had managed to get Mom to agree to at least let her take a couple of the girls to church "just to see how they liked it." Both Angela and Mary Ann succumbed to Velma's overtures and now insisted they wanted to go and see what it was. Velma left with a smile and joined her husband who was waiting patiently in the car. They both waved as they backed out of our long driveway. Mom was pissed.

Neal and I resisted like hell, though, with Neal blatantly telling Velma he'd die before he set foot in a church. I admired Neal's vehemence and tried to be just as mean about it as he was; he always said whatever he pleased and to hell with the consequences. I loved that about him, that devil-may-care attitude. He was my bad-boy hero, the one I looked up to, and I followed his lead. I wanted to be just like him, a total bad-ass, completely unafraid. We kept it up for a long time.

A few months later, and after several huge battles with Mary Ann and Angela about their hare-brained conversions, Mom found herself in church four days a week, and also converted. The girls kept coming home and telling her she was going to burn in hell, crying real tears of anguish about it. This made Mom really mad, and eventually guilty, so she went to the church just to see for herself what was going on. That's all it took.

So now it was time for Dad to resist, and it became the battle of the boys against the girls. Mom could force the younger girls to get in the car and go, but she couldn't force me and Neal, and she couldn't force Dad. We were too big by then. Dad fought them all off for several months, but finally went just to get Mom to stop crying about it all the time. And ultimately, Dad found himself going on Sunday mornings to appease Mom, and then he made Neal and I go to keep Mom happy. We were mad as hell about it. Little caterpillars, forced now to be butterflies, we were – at least according to the church. One of their hymns said we were all "worms" and were it not for Jesus, we'd never make it to heaven — we could not be remediated without God's grace! We were *lucky* to have been found and pulled into the fold, they told us. We continued to argue and fight, but the more we resisted, the more determined Mom became to force our wayward souls to the light. She'd become completely consumed by those people and their religious indoctrination.

Thus, the Pentecostal Evangelical religion invaded our family over the ensuing months, gradually violating and wrecking our sense of self as well as our family identity. Every thought and action became wrong or suspect, unless, of course, it was a nice thought about Jesus. We learned about heaven and hell and Satan and demons; we learned that we were born as terrible sinners and the devil was running us straight to the gates of hell. Every action and thought to that point in our lives, as it turned out, had been nothing but one sin after the other and we had been oh-so-foolishly unaware! Suddenly, my older sisters couldn't wear jeans or cut their hair or go out with boys. We weren't allowed to sass Mom, couldn't swim with the opposite sex, and couldn't swear — by then my most prized pastime. The thought or discussion of sex was a crime as serious as murder; so was masturbation, whatever that was; I thought it must have something to do with the exciting boner and unbelievable tickle I got when shinnying up the legs of the swing set at school, so I had to stop that. Imagining "bad" things was no different than doing bad things; we sinned by thinking. Accidentally thinking about sex when looking at a girl was the same as raping a woman. We had to pray to God constantly to have pity on us and save our worthless, wayward, inherently evil, worm-infested souls, and we had to ask Jesus to invade us and take over our minds and souls like a succubus – a brain parasite – so He could slowly take control of our thoughts and make them pure, and we *must* do it willingly because we wanted to, not just because we were scared to death to burn in Hell. HE would know the difference and throw us in Hell anyway if we tried to trick Him! We all started carrying Bibles around, even to school, and we finally became what were commonly called "holy rollers."

The next thing I knew, my new best friend was Velma's son Phil, and I was memorizing the entire New Testament for Bible Quiz competition.

We were caught. My social circle became the church and its members, and we attended every Wednesday night, Sunday morning, and Sunday night for indoctrination, and Thursday night for choir practice.

Thus, we were sucked into the powerful emotional vortex of the Assembly of God church, and it was many long years before I finally escaped. Others weren't so fortunate.

It was against this backdrop that the battle over *Rosemary's Baby* occurred one wintry Sunday night in 1970. Mom was headed off to church for evening services and decided to leave us hoodlums at home for the evening because she was sick and tired of all our bickering. Angela, being the oldest at fourteen, was in charge. Instructions were given as Mom swept out the door. Under no circumstances were we to watch the debut of *Rosemary's Baby* on TV that night, the horrific show about a baby that was the incarnation of Satan himself.

Demon possession is no joke in the Pentecostal faith, as everyone knows that demons possess the unsuspecting at every opportunity. Mom had been convinced that even the slightest exposure to such evil could weaken our little souls and allow us to be possessed, especially from such a horror as *Rosemary's Baby*. I had almost convinced myself that it was true. Visions of fangs, red skin with warts, and tiny devil horns filled my overactive imagination. Everyone was talking about this new scary film, so I had an inkling of the plot. Mom said if I opened my mind even a crack, the demons might come in.

How can an adult believe such a fantastic idea? Well, I'll tell you. Every Sunday night, one after the other, the people in the church would testify during the "testimony service," the part where individuals stand up before the sermon begins and admit to their sins and difficulties of the week. Here, they would talk about the various demons they had fought off that particular week, reporting with sincerity, and through torrents of tears, that they could at times see the vicious things wrestling over their souls in the Church aisles, red eyes bulging, horns locked in virtual combat. My ten-year-old mind couldn't imagine why these adults would report such things if they weren't true. There must truly be SOMETHING trying to sneak up on me and snatch my soul every second! Why else would these grownups cry and be so sincere if it wasn't true? And yet I doubted. I wanted to actually *see* a demon before I committed to this belief system.

So, I was very nervous this particular night, knowing this terrible program was going to be on television. Even without turning it on, I could feel the demons looming over the house as Mom walked out the front door.

Once Mom left, the battle for our souls began. Mary Ann, always the bad girl, promptly turned the TV on to ABC where she immediately found the movie in progress. Angela shrilly condemned her, invoking Jesus, and flipped the station, but

Mary Ann just flipped it back. This went on, back and forth, for a while, until we all became too intrigued by *Rosemary's Baby* and accidentally became glued to the screen. But then it got scary. The mother had apparently been fucked by Satan, the proof of which was the demonic baby being birthed right in front of us, and all of a sudden, the warnings about demons getting into us began to seem not only true, but imminent.

Angela leaped up and switched the channel. Mary Ann was scared out of her mind, but she really wanted to see what that goddamned baby was going to do next. She wanted to *see* what a demon looked like. She flipped the channel back.

"Stop it!" Angela screamed.

"No, YOU stop it!" Mary Ann screamed back. "I want to see what's gonna happen! Now leave it alone!"

"Mom said you can't watch this horrible show! I'm turning it off!" Angela hollered back.

"You touch that dial and I'll kill you!" Mary Ann screamed back.

"Mom's gonna whip you like crazy when she gets home!" Angela yelled. "I'm telling her everything you've done!"

Angela flipped it again.

Mary Ann flipped it back.

Angela couldn't take it. She grabbed Mary Ann and yanked her away from the TV, a big mistake. The next thing I knew, there was such a tangle of arms and legs and long hair mixed with screams of rage, and slaps, and scratching, that I couldn't get out of the way fast enough.

Onto the couch, against the chair, rolling on the floor, the battle went, escalating in violence. The demon baby on the TV thrashing around in the background was nothing compared to what was going on in our living room. Lamps were rattling, chairs were shaking, and books and toys were flying through the air, as though cast by a poltergeist rather than two junior high girls. I scrambled to the relative safety of Mom's favorite rocking chair and buried myself in it, alarmed and waiting for this ferocious battle to end, but it didn't. It just intensified.

Mary Ann deftly thwarted one of Angela's attack leaps, and with arms locked at the elbows, hit her open-handed square in the chest, pushing her with nuclear force straight into the toybox, the lid crashing down and slamming her on the head. Her butt was stuck hopelessly in the box and her legs were thrashing violently around over the side of the toybox, unable to get any purchase to escape. Mary Ann twirled like a she-devil and made one final death leap through the air to finish her off.

I was frozen, eyes wide, unable to move or breathe. Angela was dead for sure, I thought, as Mary Ann's flailing body flew in slow motion with one enormous leap onto her in the toybox. But Angela did the only thing left she could do, and bent her powerful legs back and kicked with all her might just as Mary Ann landed on her. There was a groan as Mary Ann went flying through the air, her red eyes, fangs, and snaky hair smoldering with the brimstone of hell (in my imagination), and crashed into the opposite wall, the very wall that Aunt Cora's dead body had been hung up on during her extrication by the undertakers seven years ago. That whole corner of the house had to be demon-possessed. Mary Ann slid into a heap on the floor, where she lay gasping for the breath that had been knocked out of her.

"Jesus Christ, she's killed her!" I thought, but I didn't dare move. Angela, her ass incarcerated in the toybox, sat stunned and blinking at the carnage around her, thinking too she'd killed Mary Ann. The house was suddenly silent save for the screeching of Rosemary's hideous baby on the TV in the background.

Mary Ann, having resurrected herself by catching her breath, unexpectedly leaped up, ran to her bedroom, and slammed the door so hard the entire house shook, her demonic strength still ripping through her veins. I helped Angela get her butt loose from the gaping maw of the toybox. She flipped her hair and marched out of the room. "She deserved it!" she yelled. "See what happens!"

Meanwhile, Mom had a great evening in Church, praying and basking in the presence of God. She came home late that night, waltzing through the door, humming and beaming, all rosy-cheeked, full of the power of Jesus, to find the house in total disarray. I was waiting for her.

"What in the world happened in HERE?" she asked as she put away her coat, looking around in astonishment at the mess. I stared at her for a moment before answering, thinking how I could delicately put it.

"You know those demons in *Rosemary's Baby?*" I asked.

"They got Mary Ann and Angela."

"Those stupid kids at school won't stop talking about Jesus and telling me I'm going to hell!" Seth griped when he got off the bus one day in ninth grade, "What the hell are they talking about?"

"Hmmm," I said. "Well, some people believe there's an invisible entity all around us watching everything we do, and if we don't cooperate, our souls will go to a place called hell where we burn in a fire that never ends. If we worship and believe in

him/it, then we'll go to a place called heaven and play harps and sing songs instead."

"That sounds unbelievably stupid," said Seth. "Like a fairy-tale."

"You would be surprised how many people believe it," I replied. "You should understand why they do, and what they believe. It will help you deal with them. "

I went to my library and pulled out The Encyclopedia of World Religions. *"Here. Read this. I know it's a big book, but it has lots of interesting pictures and history and it talks about the religious beliefs of everyone in the world. You can't understand Christianity without understanding all the rest of these belief systems as well."*

"Do you believe this stuff, Dad?"

"No. The basic core message of each religion is the same. Be a good person, be responsible, be fair, and be honest and kind and good to other people. The rest of it, the magical thinking, is unbelievable nonsense."

"The unfortunate thing is that many religious people do not abide by the basic religious directive to treat others as they themselves would like to be treated. They instead use religion to exclude and mistreat others. I think this is morally wrong, and it undermines the basic integrity of any set of religious rules. Some religious people are truly the real thing – kind, compassionate, thoughtful, helpful, nonjudgmental – but they seem to be few and far between, a fact which makes all religions useless as far as I'm concerned. You don't need a religious belief system to be a moral, spiritual human being. Thankfully, you can make your own decisions about how you want religion incorporated into your worldview when you're

older. As for me, I have my own ethics, integrity, and moral center, and they don't rely on or need an organized religious belief system to be real and effective."

BULLIES ——————

Dan Walker was a big, mean, overgrown galoot. In sixth grade, he towered a foot or two above us fourth-graders. David De Witt, his unlikely midget sidekick, was mean as hell, but too small to do anything about it unless he had someone like Dan around to do his dirty work for him, exactly like those two stupid mean boys in *A Christmas Story*. Every day they terrorized someone on the playground, knocking them down, stealing their ball, dragging them behind the school to pummel them, making them eat dirt, punching them in the balls, you name it.

I lived in fear that they'd take after me some day. They hated my brother, Neal, who openly scorned and taunted them. He could run fast and didn't care what he said to them since he knew he could get away. Plus, he could be mean as a wolverine himself when he wanted to be. They tried to catch him all the time. Occasionally they'd succeed, punching him in the stomach in the lunch line when no one was looking, pulling his ears or twisting his nipples. But he just spit and laughed in their faces and continued to taunt them. He hated them both.

Well, one day it had to happen. I was minding my own business playing with a red kickball when suddenly they appeared, Dan towering over me, blocking out the sun, with David sniggering beside him.

"Give me that ball," Dan said, a sickening sneer on his ugly face. I grabbed the ball and put it under my arm, looking up at him. "No. Get your own ball."

I had challenged the big ogre. I knew I was in for it, but I was suddenly just really pissed off at the two of them, at Dan for being such a big jerk, and David for being such a little pussy he had to run around with a big bully to protect his sneering, stupid little face.

"I SAID give me that ball!" Dan was glaring at me now. He took a step toward me and made a swipe at the ball while I danced away. "Give it!" he shouted.

"Do you really want this marvelous ball?" I said in a sweet, taunting, sarcastic voice. "I can see why you want it. It's a great ball. I'll bet you want it so bad you'll do anything to get it. Even chase it!"

And with that, I kicked that son-of-a-bitch completely out of the playground. I watched with glee as it sailed over the jungle gym, across the street and over the cars, bouncing across a lawn and behind the neighboring houses.

"Go get it if you want it so bad!" I hollered.

They were purple with rage, the two of them, tearing after me as I ran up to the teacher on duty and calmly parked myself at her side.

"Do you want something?" I smugly asked them. I turned to Mrs. Seaverns, who loved me. "Isn't it a nice day, Mrs. Seaverns? I think I'll just stand here and chat with you for the rest of recess. I noticed that Dan and David lost their ball across the street. They'll need permission to go and get it, don't you think?"

Fooled by a fourth-grader, Dan and David were apoplectic, but could do nothing about it. Mrs. Seaverns sent them on a humiliating journey across the street to get their stupid ball. I knew I'd eventually be beaten up for my audacity, and they tried it on the way into the school as we lined up to go back in for class, cutting in line to get right beside me, and using the other kids to block the view while they tried to punch me in the stomach. Of course, I just kept skipping to the front of the line, keeping my eye on the teacher and making sure I was in full sight. They eventually gave up and never actually caught me that year. I was too smart for them. The next year they were off to the middle school so I had a two-year reprieve, long enough for them to forget they wanted to kill me.

∽

"Dammit! What the hell is going on!" I said to myself, dragging out of my bunk to look out in the hall in my dorm. I ran down the hall in my underwear, looking for the source of the infernal hammering that was keeping me awake and driving me insane at midnight. It wasn't on my floor. I went down to the second floor. It wasn't there either. I gave up and went back upstairs to my room and covered my head with a pillow.

Seconds later, there was a violent banging on my door. "NOW what?" I said, as I climbed down and opened it, only to be grabbed by the throat by a gigantic football player who choked me and lifted me a foot off the floor by the neck.

*"Stop making so goddamned much noise, you faggot!" he screamed at me, eyes bulging out of his head. He choked me for a while longer until I couldn't breathe at all, then dropped me. "You fucking son-of-a-bitch!" I gasped. "It's not **me** making that noise! What sort of a goddamned idiot ARE you?!"*

I slammed the door in his face, understanding for the first time in my life exactly how easy it would be to be killed by another person's bare hands.

Time went by. Dan Walker was eventually murdered – shot in the head over a woman in a love triangle. His little sidekick became a farmer.

TONGUES OF FIRE

I was surrounded; smashed further and further into the church pew, my nose flattened, the smell of cologne and sweat filling my remaining nostril. Men sobbed, women screamed, their hands all over me; pressing me down, down, down; forcing the Holy Spirit into me through the top of my head, my back, my shoulders. The racket of their wailing was deafening. They screamed and begged God to fill me up with his Spirit! "In the name of the Father, the Son, and the Holy Ghost, let him feel Thy power, oh Lord!" they shrieked.

Four or five of them began speaking in tongues, babbling incomprehensibly, moaning and swaying, their tears splashing on my back. "Shenabala-hulababba-babbayaga-talabalai!" they hollered. "Agayaga-sheenababa-malacabba-hulabalai!" they shrieked.

"Good grief," I thought to myself. "When are these people going to get off of me and leave me alone? I'm getting a little tired of this. If The Spirit doesn't get in me pretty quick, I don't know what I'm going to do. They're killing me."

I tried to open my mind, to find God's spirit so that it would enter my brain. I assumed I would feel it, that there would be some sort of defining change. How hard could it be to be filled with The Spirit? I'd seen it happen to all sorts of people, and it didn't seem like they were even trying. They just suddenly started talking in tongues down at the altar. I had done all the required work. I was saved. I was prepared. I thought about God and Jesus constantly, day in and day out. Wasn't The Spirit supposed to just show up when the church elders decided it was time? I needed it to hurry up. I was suffocating.

I managed to turn my head enough to get some air. They'd been holding me down for a good twenty minutes. I was hot and sweaty, and young, at only eleven, to be receiving The Spirit, but there I was.

"For heaven's sake," I thought. "This is never going to end. I wonder what time it is? I'm really tired. Maybe I should just fake it. I wonder if they would know?"

I waited a minute. No Spirit invaded me. I sighed.

"I give up," I thought.

I rustled up some tears, and pushing myself up against their enraptured hands with all my might, I began hollering in tongues at the top of my lungs, perfectly mimicking the adults all around me.

"Hallelujah!" they all screamed in unison. "Praise God! Hullabulla-cullalullajedakadi! Thank you, Lord! Another child filled with your Spirit! Thank you, Jesus!"

"Now get off of me," I thought. "And hurry up about it, for Christ's sake." I dried my tears and went back to my seat.

Young Reverend Parker was really wound up for the Sunday night service. Having just graduated from Central Bible College's seminary school, the new Reverend had a lot to prove. Sweating and hollering, he strode across the altar, arms gesticulating, screaming into the microphone.

"Someone here is wrestling with a demon at this very moment! I can feel it! You're struggling and struggling, trying to overcome it, but Satan won't let you! You need help! I can sense it!"

He closed his eyes, walking into the audience, arms out, sensing the demon's presence with his antenna-like fingers. People prayed and moaned, weeping in the pews. "Save them Lord! Save the poor soul!" they cried.

Across the aisle he went, feeling, feeling, and suddenly... he opened his eyes to where God had led him, looking straight into the face of... Oh no! Not Tammy Phillips!

Now, I went to school with Tammy, and I knew her well. She'd been in special ed since kindergarten, but Mr. Parker didn't know that, having just arrived as the new pastor. God hadn't yet told him the entire family was dumber than a box of rocks. Her brother, Ricky, was in my class and was seriously a complete idiot, failing or nearly failing every class. Years later, his claim to fame would be that he (seriously) ran for President of the United States as a Republican, too stupid to know that he was too stupid for the job.

"So THAT'S what's wrong with her," I muttered to myself. "And all this time I just thought she was dumb. Augh, these demons are just everywhere these days."

I leaned over to my friend, Phil. "Oh my God, Phil, its Tammy!" I hissed. "She's demon-possessed! That explains everything!" Phil didn't think it was funny. He began to pray for her, ignoring my side commentary.

By now the Reverend was fully wound up. Grabbing Tammy by the head with both hands, Reverend Parker called on God to suck the demons out of her. Tammy, shrieking bloody murder, was scared out of her wits. The louder she screamed, the louder Reverend Parker screamed, thinking her shrieks were coming straight from the demon in the depths of her body, rather than just her poorly comprehending mind. I watched entranced, waiting for a hideous demon to come out of her throat. Maybe I'd finally get to see one after all. He pulled her out of the pew, now gripping her head like a vise as she screamed and cried, now swinging her around, hair flying; and then both of them suddenly lost their balance, with Tammy falling, dragging Mr. Parker over the pew and onto the floor where he landed with a thud on top of her.

Then... silence.

Everyone leaned forward in their pews, craning their necks; was the demon exorcised, or not?

Suddenly, Reverend Parker leaped up like a jack-in-the-box — boing! — hands in the air. "Pray-ise GAAWWD-uh, the de-a-mon is GAWNE!" he screamed. The crowd burst into cheers and a chorus of hallelujahs as Tammy, brushing herself off, managed to stumble to her feet, eyes glazed, weeping, and checking for broken bones.

I watched in bemusement. "I know just how you feel, Tammy," I said to myself.

S-E-X ————————————————

In the late '60s, '70s and '80s any properly educated kid
worth his salt could give a detailed anatomical and physio-
logical description of the penis, vas deferens, prostate gland,
seminal vesicles, semen, scrotum, testicles, epididymis, ova-
ries, fallopian tubes, ova, uterus, vagina, labia, clitoris, cor-
pus luteum, zygote, embryo, and placenta by seventh grade,
thanks to the cultural revolution of the '60s, hippies, femi-
nists, contraception, and the search for truth and knowledge
and social progress through better education. By the '90s we
were back to the early '60s again though, and now we're back
to the Middle Ages in regard to sex education, or at least the
McCarthy Era, but that's how things go when religious belief
takes over the culture. Any idiot can screw, of course; they
do it all the time. In fact, I think a person could fuck if all
they had was a brainstem. The problem is that sex isn't just
about fucking, and that's why a thorough education on sexual anatomy, physiology, ethics, relationships, and psycholo-
gy is essential for the modern-day human. Sex, gender, and
sexuality are three of many examples where the ideology of
"everything I need to know is in the Bible" is clearly demon-
strated to be utter hogwash. So is the ideology "the Bible is
the only source of truth." Not so, my dear.

I really knew way less about sex, though, than I should have
in the early '70s, even though it was all around me. My parents

were not progressive, and we didn't talk about it at school or at home, at least not in any sensible way. (In my school there was an optional sex education class available sometime around the senior year, a bit late to be of much use.) Sometimes conversations at home accidentally alluded to sex, but they were quickly turned to a safer topic as soon as possible.

My very first memory of my penis: I'm very, very small, and Dad has placed me in the shower with him to get me washed up while he cleans up after a day in the fields. I must be four. I look up and see his huge cock and balls hovering over me. I look down at my own tiny penis which had instantly become hard as a rock at the sight of my dad's big dick, and it stuck straight out. I had a fantastic sensation at the same time, but was also unexpectedly filled with shame and humiliation, hoping Dad wouldn't see it. He started washing me about then, soaping me up and rubbing me all over, and my dick went out of control, throbbing and hard as diamond. I thought something was wrong with me and tried to cover it up, but Dad saw it anyway. "What's going on there?" he asked in a tone of disbelief. "I don't know," I weakly replied, thinking I was in trouble. And then he said, "That shouldn't be doing that." I covered it up with my two hands for the rest of the shower and made sure he never saw it again.

For decades I didn't know what he meant by saying that, though I imagine I do now. A boy is not supposed to have such a reaction from looking at another male. The second unstated message was that erections were simply not supposed to be happening at all in small boys. Until I was about nine, I thought there was something wrong with me. My dick was hard all the time! Did I have a disease? Was this going to kill me eventually? I finally asked Neal if his did the same thing, and he admitted that it did, which gave me some relief. If it happened to both of us, it seemed less likely there was something wrong with me or that it would kill me, since maybe it was happening to other boys and I just didn't know it, but certainly none had died at school yet. And then finally one day, a miracle. My fourteen-year-old uncle was visiting and staying over for a week or two. We boys went to our room to change into swimming trunks to go to town and swim. My uncle looked like a man already, and I again developed a "boner," as we called them back then, simply at the thought of seeing my uncle naked. I was just ten and had seen only Dad and my brother naked, having not spent time in a locker room yet. So, imagine my surprise when my uncle pulled off his pants to reveal a gigantic boner, pubic hair, and big balls. I nearly fainted. He was fourteen and had a boner! *He* was alive! He didn't even look sick! It MUST be okay to have a boner! And then, again, that same feeling I had back when I was four staring up at my dad's big dick, only this time I had a remote sense of what it meant. I became very talkative and kept trying to look at my uncle's dick, and finally went out on a limb and asked why it was so huge. He just laughed at me. Later that night, before I went to sleep, I got up the nerve to ask him about boners, and he told me with absolute certainty that "no, there is nothing wrong with you – you're supposed to have boners." Sweet relief; nothing was ever the same again. This thing was meant to be enjoyed, whatever it was. I wasn't sick, I wasn't dying, and it wasn't bad.

For the next two years, Neal and I shamelessly examined and compared our dicks at every opportunity we had, hard

and soft. His was bigger, but he was almost two years older, and we had by now surmised that eventually mine would
catch up and they would both become HUGE, and we couldn't
wait. We knew they felt really good when they were hard, but
we didn't know why exactly, or how they were supposed to
be used on people. We had some ideas from watching the
animals, but it seemed a bit far-fetched that people could be
THAT much like animals, climbing all over each other and
pumping away like that. It seemed too gross to believe. But
by this time the kids at school were talking about "jacking off"
and "hard-ons" and "pussies" and "getting some" and "pieces
of ass," none of which I could quite figure out, but knowing
that it had something to do with my dick.

Inevitably, one or the other of us had to find out the truth,
but how it happened was hardly a planned event. Yes, my
brother and I stole my sisters' book entitled *Your Changing Body*, thinking that it would somehow help us figure out
what we were supposed to do with our wives when we grew
up and had carnal knowledge, but it only told us about growing breasts and menstruating every month, something that
we knew more about than we cared to know already with our
older sisters around. And when we asked Dad or Mom directly about sex, they simply ho-hummed around and told us we
were too young to know any of that stuff. So needless to say,
all this secrecy simply made us crazy for information – we
wanted to KNOW! The chatter at school was getting more
and more graphic, and I didn't believe anything the kids were
saying could possibly be true.

So, one day Neal and I were sitting in the front seat of the
pickup as Dad took the back roads to the Des Moines River bottom, where he had a farm. The river bottom is the land along

the river; it's flat and generally rich, and Dad liked to go down there and work, and knock down trees, and clear the land for more fields. Neal loved to go along to ride on the tractor or bulldozer. I loved to go along to wander near the water's edge and see what sort of creatures I could capture and bring home, though this could be dangerous on the Des Moines River. One time I started to step into the water to look at something when I suddenly saw a huge beaver trap, my foot hovering above the pedal that would release it and cause it to snap my leg off. I had seen smaller traps, but never a huge beaver trap, so it's a wonder I realized the danger I was in and didn't just step right into it. I was only about six at the time. No one would ever have found me if I had, as I was way off in the banks of the river and would probably have succumbed to my injury by the time anyone ever found me. Near-death experiences aside, I loved going to the river bottom.

Dad thought it was about time I took more of an interest in his work since I was supposed to grow up to be a farmer. He didn't like it that Mom had taught me to knit and sew, and he didn't like it that I always had my nose in an encyclopedia or was outside studying plants and animals. Every time he saw me, he'd yell, "Why don't you do something constructive for a change? Get your nose out of that stupid book and do some work, would you? Why aren't you interested in farming? You're never going to amount to a fart in a windstorm if you don't cut it out! Shape up and pay attention! You're pathetic!" He knew I was going along with him only to play by the river, but I guess he thought at least some of the farming stuff would eventually rub off on me if he forced me to ride on the tractor once in a while, or at least smell some diesel exhaust.

We were flying at high speed over the hills on the gravel road, something we always begged Dad to do since it gave us "tickle tummies," when for some reason, Neal opened the glove box and pulled out a book. He was bored of course, so was just rummaging around. He flipped open the book, and all of a sudden, there it was; the answer. Yes, it was in black and white, but there was no doubt about it. Men and women actually doing it – on chairs, in beds, standing up, sitting down – it was amazing. And I couldn't believe it.

We flipped through page after page, Dad ignoring us and listening to the market reports. I had the oddest sensation in the pit of my stomach as I looked at the pictures in this book, and then that sensation again down lower in my pelvis. I looked at Neal; by this time, at nearly twelve, he was getting pubic hair and his dick had reached alarming proportions; I could see it straining mightily against his pants. Mine was doing the same, even without any pubic hair. My eyes were glued to the pages, shocked by the enormous dicks disappearing into the pussies I never quite understood until just that moment. How did they fit??? How did they make themselves get a boner so they could do it? Would my dick get THAT big someday? I couldn't see enough fast enough. We started whispering excitedly as we flipped through the pages, "Look at that!" "Wow!" "Is that real?" "Do they really get that big?" "Oh my God, is that what we have to do?" Now we finally knew why we woke up with "boners" in the morning; it was practice for the real thing.

Sensing the sudden flurry of activity beside him, Dad happened to glance down for a second and see what we had in our hot little hands, and without a moment's hesitation grabbed the book and threw it back in the glove box.

"Hey!" Neal said. "We weren't done with that!" "Yeah," I chimed in as Neal, gripping his crotch in agony, grabbed the book again from the glove box.

But Dad took the book and threw it back in the glove box and got really mad. The cat was out of the bag, and he was subjected to one question after another by the two of us, questions that he was ill-prepared to handle. He declared me to be too young to know any of "this stuff," being only ten, but figured Neal was old enough to know at twelve, so he finally relinquished and with great difficulty did his best to explain sex. By the time he was done, I was so confused and grossed out that it would be impossible for me to think about it for years without nearly getting sick.

I never looked at anyone the same again. I imagined them all doing it, all those grownups; and all the kids would, horror of horrors, grow up and do it too. "Except me," I thought to myself. "I'll never do it!"

It turned out, of course, that my parents were doing it all the time, right under my nose, my foolish little mind having been too uninformed to know what was going on. I suddenly realized that my parents were sexual beings; that every time Dad came in from the fields at noon and told Mom it was "time to go have a conference," it was code for sex; every time I heard that rhythmic bed-squeaking from down the hall as I was drifting off to sleep, they were having sex; and that one time when Dad sauntered out of the bedroom with only a towel, casting about, looking for a chair, they were having sex. "Oh my God," I thought. "My mom and dad are having sex every day and every night!"

Of course, Neal and I told our older sisters what we suspected and after a lot of discussion we decided our suspicions had to be correct; there simply was no other explanation for the frequent disappearances into a bedroom with all doors closed. The evidence had been right under our noses the whole time. We knew to leave them alone when they went to the bedroom but didn't know they were there to do THAT. I had made the mistake once of walking in and finding mom on top of dad, with both under the sheets, but the fierceness of their "get out!" was enough to make sure it never happened again. I couldn't figure out what they were doing and thought it was a really weird way to sleep.

Meanwhile, back at school, I shared my newfound misinformation from Dad with my friends; turns out his description was so confusing I didn't know what organ went where, thus creating a bit of a headache for a lot of moms and dads when their fifth-grade kids came home and repeated what I had told them about sex. Their parents weren't much better than mine, but at least they came back to school knowing what organ went with the other, and straightened me out.

"Oh," I mused. "Well, maybe that's not quite as gross as I thought, but it's still gross."

We began using the showers and locker rooms after P.E. and sports that year, in fifth grade, and for the first time, we boys saw each other naked. Some were really shy about it while others were whooping it up, flooding the showers, and sliding on their bare asses across the floor. Penis size and pubic hair were the big topics of conversation, and pointed comparisons were made and discussed with intense interest.

It was about this time that Neal, two years older, started masturbating constantly. I don't know how he learned how to do it. We never talked about it, but I could hear him really getting after it every night as soon as the lights were off, though I didn't understand exactly what he was doing. Soon enough, of course, I deduced the technique by quietly listening to and watching the conversations of all the boys at school; there were enough hints to assume the technique. So, I started too. Nothing came out, but it felt good anyway. Neal told me that he was making a lot of sperm, and it felt REAL-LY good when you had sperm to shoot out. I couldn't wait to be older.

It must have been about this time when a really bad thing happened one day, though I could never articulate or understand exactly what about it had been so awful until decades later. I had blocked it from my mind until I was in the throes of writing this chapter in this book. Dad came in from the field to the house and said he needed us boys to help him do something. "Where's Neal?" he asked. "In our room, I think," I said.

"Well, let's go get him," he said, "and I'm going to need you outside too." So, we went there to get Neal first, and the door was shut, and Dad just walked in and found Neal with a huge hard-on jacking off on the top bunk. Rather than apologizing and closing the door, he walked right up to Neal, who had yanked up the covers as fast as he could, and pulled the covers back off him, exposing his hard cock. Neal yanked the covers up again, and Dad yanked them down again and began mocking him, asking him what he was doing. By this time, Neal was furious and starting to cry, trying to turn over to hide his exposed dick, but Dad kept yanking him back to humiliate him, even grabbing his cock and sarcastically mocking him with, "Oh, so you want to just play with this all the time instead of working, huh, is that it? Is that it? You just want to play with this?" He yanked on it so hard

I thought he was seriously trying to pull his cock off. I was frozen watching this scene, and thinking about it now, I am flooded with anxiety and my heart is pounding. I was so angry at Dad I wanted to kill him. I was filled with rage and anxiety and fear for Neal. I was embarrassed for Neal, and I was erotically turned on by the sight of the physical altercation between these two men, the one forcing the other to keep his gigantic throbbing cock in full view of all three of us in spite of all his efforts to escape. "Stop it! Stop it, stop it, stop it!" I yelled. I had never been so sexually aroused or so conflicted and freaked out as I was at that moment. I was horrified and crying, yet with a raging erection of my own, completely not understanding what the hell was happening in that room at that moment, or with my own body.

Everything in that scene was wrong: the verbal abuse, the physical assault, and the cognitive dissonance between my fear, anxiety, tears, and my own erection. There was something to be learned there, but I was too freaked out to get it. It was just one more act of terrorism by my dad, one that so altered the landscape of my reality that I just had to forget it ever happened. But Neal didn't. He wept and wept that night, and for the first time in his life, he was cowed by his own father.

It's 2001. Fourteen-year-old Seth sat staring at the computer screen as I walked into my library after a long day of surgery.

"Hey, Seth. How's it going?"

"Good. Hey Dad..."

"What?"

"I know you think you've told me everything about sex, but what's a cock ring?"

I paused. I had always answered every question the boys asked me from the first day they could actually talk. If I didn't know the answer, I would look it up with them. It didn't matter how dicey the topic and it didn't matter their age when they asked me. Any question about sex was just like any other topic and was directly answered. I'd pretty much seen and heard everything by now from all my patients (you can't EVEN begin to imagine) so most of the time I just shrugged and gave the appropriate response without thinking twice about it. Though this question gave me temporary pause; I was actually surprised by it.

"Well, it's a ring that men put around their penis and scrotum that tightens as they get an erection, holding the blood in so they stay erect longer and enjoy sex more. Why are you asking me this? It's for older guys, not young ones."

"Could you get me one?"

Sam, eleven, from the other room, "Yeah, Dad, could you get me one too?"

"No! Are you insane? That's the last thing either one of you needs! Why do you guys even know about all this stuff? I never even heard of a cock ring until I was forty years old! Good grief! Now stop asking me for such crazy things! You're just doing it to watch me freak out!"

Seth just laughed at me. "I didn't really want one, Dad. Just teasing you!"

The next week I went and bought for them the Kama Sutra, The Joy of Sex, and a number of medical grade educational videotapes on how to have great sex and great sexual relationships. Then we talked about sex with special emphasis on why *it's important to wait until the time is right. Then I filled a drawer with condoms, just in case they ever succumbed – God forbid – to their inevitable biological destiny.*

BURNING DOWN
THE HOUSE

"David – come in the bathroom a second. I think I smell smoke in there."

Mary Ann grabbed my arm.

"Oh, you do not! For heaven's sake, Mary Ann, why would you smell smoke in the bathroom? How would it get in there?" I complained. "Can't you see I'm busy reading?"

It was a lazy Sunday winter afternoon; everyone was reading, napping, or quietly dinking around the house; Mom and Dad were asleep after a romp, and Mary Ann was, as usual, making herself beautiful in the bathroom, attending to such important matters as making her hair gigantic and applying just the right amount of makeup. It didn't matter she was only fifteen.

Mary Ann was insistent. I begrudgingly put my book aside and let her drag me into the bathroom. "I don't smell anything," I said. "No – over here," Mary Ann replied as she directed me to the cabinets beside the toilet. "I smell smoke over here." I took a big breath; I smelled it too, just a trace of acrid smoke. "That's sort of weird," I said. "Why would we smell smoke here? There's nothing here to catch on fire." I paused. "Wait a minute; this set of shelves here has a door on the bottom that opens to the basement so you can get to the bathtub plumbing behind it. You don't suppose something's on fire in the basement, do you?"

"Oh my God," Mary Ann whispered. "Hurry, let's go see!"

We ran through the house to the top of the stairs and flipped the light on. "I don't see anything; no fire, no smoke. I don't smell anything either," I said. "Let's go on down."

We tentatively crept down the stairs. The basement looked normal. It was a really long basement, filling the entire space below the large ranch-style house we called home. We headed toward the far end where the furnace and water heater stood. "I still don't see anything. This doesn't really make any sense; if we smelled smoke upstairs, we should be able to see it right here under the bathro ... wait!"

My eye caught a flicker of light off to my right; I heard voices. I turned quickly, grabbing Mary Ann's arm. The opening to the crawl space under Mom and Dad's bedroom was alight with flames – tall, orange, hot tongues greedily licking at the dry wood of the floor joists directly under their bed.

I couldn't understand the scene; it just didn't make sense. There was absolutely nothing in the crawl space that could catch fire – not even any wiring in that location. It was just a big dirt pile under that part of the house, walled off from the rest of the basement but still connected by an opening, high up on the wall, to keep the temperature above freezing. It was through that opening that we could see the flames.

We reflexively screamed, "Fire! Fire! The house is on fire!" as we wheeled about and raced for the stairs, braking to a screeching halt when behind us we suddenly heard screaming and crying. We turned just in time to see Kathy flying through the air after leaping from the ledge of the crawl space, Julie scrambling close on her heels onto the ledge, perching like a little monkey for a fraction of a second before she, too, launched herself into the air, landing lithely on her little feet on the cement five feet below. They ran to our sides.

At that moment, I stopped. "What were you two girls doing in there? What's on fire? Were you playing with matches?" This was no time to be having a discussion, but I I needed to know the precise mechanism of the fire as I began analyzing a way out of it.

"We put a box on a candle, because we didn't want anyone to know we had a candle in there, and the box caught on fire," Kathy whimpered, scared out of her wits. We could see the flames getting brighter and brighter.

I realized at that point we might have a chance of putting it out, but we needed help. I figured it would take a couple minutes for the fire to get a strong hold on the wood and the main fire was simply in the box. Boxes always burn really fast and hot. "Let's get Dad, quick!" I shouted.

We ran up the stairs, the four of us, screaming loud enough to wake the dead, barging into Mom and Dad's bedroom where, thankfully, they were actually napping, their daily "conference" long since over.

"The house is on fire! The house is on fire!" we screamed. "Come quick! It's in the basement! Mary Ann smelled smoke in the bathroom and we went downstairs and there's a big fire in the crawl space! Kathy and Julie accidentally started it with a candle and a box! Quick! We might be able to put it out!"

Dad threw on his overalls and ran with Mary Ann and me to the basement stairs. Mom threw on a dress and started rounding up the rest of the kids, jerking them into the living room and grabbing handfuls of clothes, coats, and boots. Angela, the oldest, ran from her room to see what the commotion was and then to the stairs to help us. Neal appeared from someplace as well, and we all took the stairs two at a time to face our hungry enemy which, by now, was beginning to truly devour the floor joists.

While Mom prepared Kathy, Julie, Sandy, and Ev for a rapid escape upstairs, Dad quickly assessed the situation downstairs. "Grab that bucket, David, quick!" I flew to the corner, grabbed it and threw it to him. He opened the spigot on the side of the water boiler and rapidly filled the bucket, racing to the crawl space and heaving the contents over the edge onto the flames, slowing them significantly. "Grab another bucket! There's one in the garage!" he hollered. Neal galloped up the stairs. Mom's voice came floating down: "Angela! I need some help up here! Get to the phone and call the fire department!" Angela took the stairs two at a time, leaving me, Dad, Mary Ann, and Neal to fight the fire.

Dad ran back to the boiler to refill his bucket as the flames grew back to their original strength. Neal ran up behind him with another bucket. "Neal, fill that bucket as fast as you can as soon as I'm done with this one, and bring it to me right away!"

I ran upstairs to help Mom, who was crying and collecting kids, tying bonnets and shoes, putting on boots. All the little girls were crying because Mom was scared and crying. Angela was on the phone with the fire department. Mom started barking orders at me to get this and that and throw it in the car. "We've got to get out of here before the house fills with smoke," she said in a quavering voice, to no one in particular.

About that time, we heard Dad. "Eleanor! We've put it out! The fire's out! We don't have to leave!" He, Neal, and Mary

Ann had formed a bucket brigade using the water from the boiler/radiator system, dousing the flames repeatedly until they finally went out. The fire had indeed begun consuming the floor joists, requiring Dad to climb into the crawl space and do a careful inspection to make certain there were no glowing wood fibers remaining. The fire truck arrived and the local firemen took a good look around, declared the house safe, and congratulated Dad for organizing a quick response. Only then did Mom feel safe enough to defrock the kids and throw her emotionally drained body into the rocking chair, sighing in tremendous relief.

Dad came upstairs finally. "Where's that Kathy and Julie?" he said in a menacing tone. "What were they trying to do, burn me to death in my own bed? Stupid idiots! I oughtta beat the living daylights out of them. Don't they have a lick of brains in their heads?"

Mom glared at him. "You leave those girls alone, Johnny. They're scared to death as it is; I put them to bed, and you just never mind. I think they're well aware of the damage they almost did. I don't want to hear a word out of you, and you keep your hands off of them. They're only little girls, and they've suffered enough without you making matters worse."

Dad started to argue; "Well, I think...."

"I DON'T CARE WHAT YOU THINK, JOHNNY COSTER! I said leave those kids alone, and I MEAN IT!"

Aside from a stern lecture to all of us about the dangers of playing with fire, that was pretty much the end of it. Of course, we accidentally caught a couple of barns on fire and started grassfires that got out of control a few times, but other than that we pretty much followed Mom's instructions.

Ironically, Dad himself caught the house on fire a few

years later, when not paying attention to his wood-burning stove. He put that one out too, of course. He could do anything.

❧

Man, how I hated this part of my surgery training. In 1988 Iowa Methodist had created a Burn Unit and hired a burn specialist to take care of victims in central Iowa. It was a necessary addition to our training, and I ultimately was assigned to six months on the burn/reconstructive plastics rotation, way more time than anyone else. I wanted to learn all about it, but it was a heavy burden to bear.

The patients here in the unit suffered more than any other patients in the entire hospital system, if they lived to tell about it. A burn trauma would be called through the pager system, and I would run to the emergency room, often finding a patient with horrific third-degree burns. They would be charred, coughing up smoke. Getting an IV was terribly difficult through burned skin, so cut-downs had to be used to find veins. Once stabilized, they were transferred to the unit. Here, supportive critical care was performed, including cleaning and scraping the burned areas in a big tub of water. This process was unbelievably painful, and if the patient survived the next three days, the "tubbing" had to be done regularly, with high doses of morphine.

After a few days, they would be taken to the operating room for debridement (excision) of the burns. This would either be partial or complete excision, depending upon the depth of the burns. We would then "harvest" skin from unburned areas using an oscillating blade that removed just the top layers, mesh it so it could be stretched to cover more surface area, and then place it on the freshly excised burn areas. The process was painfully tedious, and the care required after with dress-

ing changes, antibiotics, IV fluids, nutrition supplementation, pain and anxiety medications, physical therapy, and psychotherapy was intense.

I found working in there emotionally devastating. Many patients died early from lung damage due to inhaling smoke and hot gases. Others died from sepsis. Others died due to the overall physiologic insult of massive burns which destroyed nearly all their skin, the largest organ of the human body. Some we saved, but their scars were both a constant pain and a constant reminder of what had happened to them. They would never really get over it.

From this, I learned a lot about plastic and reconstructive skin surgery, and a lot about emotional interactions with patients. I learned that, sometimes, for my own protection, it was better to wear my objective-surgeon hat than wear my emotionally connected compassionate-human hat. A surgeon can't be a surgeon if they feel too much at the wrong time.

ANIMAL HOUSE

"David," Nancy whispered loudly to me as we passed in the hallway at school.

"What?" I whispered back, suspecting some sort of conspiracy was in the air.

"Mickey Hinmon is spreading rumors that we keep livestock in the house! She's told all sorts of people we live like hillbillies. She even said we keep cows and pigs in the house! Everyone's talking about it!"

I thought for a moment. Why would she say a thing like that? It's not true, so what could have given her that impression? I mean, gee, we have a lot of pets, but that doesn't mean we keep livestock in the house. Who would keep livestock in the house? Is she nuts?

I went and found Mickey.

"Mickey, I hear you're telling people that the Costers keep livestock in the house. Why are you telling such a ridiculous story?"

Mickey was surprised to be accosted directly like this. She stuttered for a moment, and then replied, "Well, someone who stayed overnight at your house one time said that you had chickens in your bedroom."

I hesitated for a second. Her statement was, well, technically true.

"Mickey, those were baby chickens I was hatching in an

incubator, not grown chickens running around the room. There's a big difference. I simply hatched them in the incubator so I could take them outside and put them in the brooder house. I do it in my bedroom all the time so I can keep a close eye on the eggs and make sure there is no problem with the temperature and humidity. They have to be turned twice a day and watched carefully."

"Oh," said Mickey. "They said they were all over your room, running around."

"Are you crazy, Mickey? How could a person live with chickens crapping all over his room and perching on the bedposts at night? How could you believe such a stupid story?"

"Well! I didn't know! You guys always have such crazy things going on out there! That's why I believed it!"

"Okay, fine, Mick. But stop telling everyone we keep livestock in the house. It's not true, and you know it. And I want you to go and tell all the people that you've told this story to that it isn't true, okay? I'm really mad about this, and so's Nancy."

"All right," Mickey said. "I'm sorry."

Of course, there *was* the time we brought the goat into the dining room just to see what it would do, and well, the other time when we coaxed Kathy's horse Babe to go up the porch stairs and partway into the house before Mom heard it and came flying out of the kitchen to shoo us all out. And I guess my parakeets were allowed to fly about inside pretty much as they pleased, living on the top bookshelf in my room when not in their cage. And we did let the ferrets play loose in the living room, and, well, you know.

We indeed had a lot of pets. Let's see: goats, goldfish, crawdads, bullfrogs, toads, snakes, tropical fish, parakeets, canaries, turtles, rabbits, guinea pigs, ferrets, dogs, cats, exotic chickens, quail, ducks, geese, guineas, horses, piglets, pigeons, and an occasional rescued wild bird or animal.

We acquired our first raccoon, Pepper, quite by accident one day. Neal and I went to the granary with Tippy, our dog, to play and see what sort of mischief we could get into. We were about to climb the ladder to the upper level when we heard Tippy barking frantically inside the grain storage area. It sounded like he was running around in there; we could hear his nails scratching the cement, and a lot of scrambling.

There was a hole cut in the wall about the size of our heads, so we ran over to look in and see what was going on. Just as Neal approached the hole, a baby raccoon popped out of it, looking frantic. It glanced around, decided that we looked safer than the snarling dog behind it, and took a flying leap, landing squarely on top of Neal's head. Tippy's snapping jaws came blasting through the hole a half second later, desperate to get the coon. He couldn't get through the hole though, so he disappeared and ran out the other side of the barn and raced back into the alley.

Meanwhile, Neal stood there with a coon on his head. It was gripping his skull tightly, but otherwise seemed unfazed by our presence, neither angry nor frightened. Neal just stood still, not knowing if he'd be attacked or bitten; this wasn't an everyday occurrence. The coon was really, really small – just a baby. About then, Tippy came charging back in, causing the poor little coon to begin clawing and scrambling about on Neal's head, looking for an escape route. I grabbed the dog by the scruff and dragged him away; the coon settled down again in Neal's hair. We decided to walk carefully to the house, me dragging the dog, Neal sporting the coon.

I managed to get Tippy to settle down as I dragged him to the house, beating him and telling him "no!" every time he turned to look at our coon. He was a smart dog, and by the time we got to the house, he realized we meant business; he was to leave the coon alone whether or not he wanted to.

Mom was out back in the garden picking tomatoes when we appeared. "Mom! Mom! Look what we've got! We got a baby coon! And he's already tame! Tippy was trying to get him and he jumped on Neal's head to escape!" Mom stood up from where she was bending over a particularly fruitful to-mato vine, hands on her hips. "Oh, isn't he cute!" she chortled with a mix of surprise and glee. "Look at him sitting on your head!" she laughed. "That's the funniest thing I've ever seen!" and she laughed until she cried.

She picked up the apple basket she was using to collect to-matoes, bringing it over to us. "Here, put him in this; it'll keep the dog from seeing him and maybe he won't be so scared. What are you going to name him?"

"You mean we get to keep him, Mom? Really? Good! Good! We have a pet baby coon! Oh, isn't he cute? Look at him in his basket! Look at his little hands and his cute little mask!"

"I think you should name him Pepper," Mom said. "His fur looks like pepper."

And that was how we acquired our first raccoon. He was a fantastic pet, tame from the start, easy-tempered, and abso-lutely hilarious. He snuggled in bed with us; woke us with his soft, probing little hands, tickling our necks and faces; stole cookies from the cookie jar; chased us in the yard when we played tag; rode in the car with us to town; and let us dress him up in baby clothes. We had the best summer with Pepper.

About the time we started back to school, though, Pepper began to have a wanderlust, disappearing for a few days at a time, then reappearing, each time seeming a little more standoffish than he'd been the time before.

When cold weather hit, Pepper was gone. We missed him terribly, but Mom explained to us that he had to go and hibernate someplace and would eventually need to be with his own kind rather than with us, which we accepted but still hoped he'd come back. The following spring, he reappeared once, big and fuzzy, but he wouldn't play with us. He hung around for a few hours before moving on once and for all.

A few years later, we acquired another baby coon in a similar fashion, again involving a dog and a barn, but Rascal didn't jump on anyone's head.

Rascal, like Pepper, proved to be incredibly tame. Unlike Pepper, he had a stubborn side that was intractable, and a social side that was hilarious and eventually problematic. We had a new puppy, Major, a German Shepherd/Collie mix, Dad having dispatched Tippy with a bullet to the head after he sequentially attacked and bit several people, including my uncle who very nearly lost his eye out of the deal. Rascal and Major were the best of friends from the start, playing on the living room carpet, leaping, mock attacking, rolling and tussling head over heels.

Rascal saw no need to find his own kind when he got older. As a matter of fact, he decided the house was his. Thus, we found him opening the refrigerator and cupboards, rummaging around for some lunch, or sitting on his butt on the kitchen counter with his lower legs splayed around the cookie jar, lid off, his mouth full of chocolate chip cookies. This wouldn't have been such a big deal, perhaps, but Rascal really got big. He must have weighed thirty pounds by autumn, a weight that made it debatable as to who was really in charge. We often couldn't control him; if he wanted the cookies, for instance, it was all we could do to get the cookie jar away from him, he gripped it so tightly. Nor could we keep him from opening any door he pleased. He came in and out of the house, got into closets, and took whatever he wanted. Sometimes he took things outside and we never saw them again. Like Pepper, he wandered more and more; however, he always came back, bigger and fatter than ever, looking for his family and letting himself in the house. Mom took to locking the door to keep him out, but somehow, he still managed to find ways to get in about half the time.

I still recall one particularly bad episode when Dad opened the front door thinking someone had knocked. As the door swung in, so did Rascal, in all his gigantic glory. Dad, quick as a wink, grabbed him by the back of the neck and attempted to toss him out, but there was no going there! Rascal grabbed the door frame with all his might and couldn't be pried off. Attempting to unlock Rascal's fingers, Dad lost his grip on his neck, and the darned coon scrambled behind the armoire. Dad went after him; Rascal went up the window screen, leaped to a lamp, knocked it over with a crash and squeezed behind the couch. Dad moved the couch; Rascal climbed over it and ran into the back bedroom. After an hour of moving furniture and watching Rascal break everything, we gave up on catching him and decided to trick him by pretending to ignore him, a tactic that always made him come out to see what we were doing. Sure enough, an hour later, he sauntered out to see what was up. Dad nabbed him with a bear hug, I opened the front door, and Dad coon-tossed him a good twenty feet, slamming the door before he hit the ground.

There were a few more break-ins after that, but as winter approached, they became less and less frequent and eventually stopped. We figured Rascal had gone back to the wild.

The following May, we were in the living room watching TV one evening when there was a big crash in the dining room. We all turned in time to see some ceiling tiles fall on the floor by the china hutch. A little raccoon rear end was scrambling to get back into the ceiling. We jumped up and ran to the dining room to find two baby raccoons sitting on the carpet, looking around in surprise amidst the ceiling rubble.

Apparently, Rascal was a girl, not a boy. She'd managed to pry open the air vent of the cupola on the roof and move into the attic where, unbeknownst to us, she'd spent the winter and given birth to a half-dozen babies.

We picked the babies up and took them to the hallway where the attic access was located and gave them back to their mother, who was waiting patiently a few feet away. Mom had previously declared there'd be no more coons in the house, ever. As far as she was concerned, enough was enough; but upon seeing Rascal again she decided she'd let her raise her little ones in the attic, especially considering the fight we were likely to get into trying to pry her out of there.

Every night after that the baby raccoons watched TV with us, their little eyes gleaming from the dining room ceiling where they poked their heads through to see what we were doing.

In midsummer, I was awakened around eleven o'clock one night by the sound of raccoons chirring outside my window. Rascal was quietly coaxing her youngsters off the roof and onto an apple tree branch that eventually would lead them to the ground. I watched them silently as they chattered and disappeared in the moonlight. The next morning, I climbed onto the roof and nailed the grate back over the cupola, sawed the offending branch off the apple tree, and that was the end of that.

CHARLOTTE ───────────

God only knows why it was wandering around at the end of the driveway, rooting in the grass – but there it was – a little lost piglet. We were all waiting for the school bus, and we could see it coming up the road – it was already at Whitis's. We had only a minute or two to figure out what to do.

"Hand it to me; I'll take it to the house," Mary Ann said as I manhandled the squealing thing. It was really cute: pink with white fur, about the size of a half-grown cat. "I wonder where it came from."

"I don't know, but it's mine," I replied. "I caught it first."

"It is not!" everyone hollered at once. After a quick battle, we decided that we'd have to share this new pet. Mary Ann turned on her heel and ran with it to the house.

The pig was named Charlotte by the time Mary Ann was halfway up the drive, after the spider in *Charlotte's Web*, and was shortly thereafter snuggled into a box in the utility room where she was left for the day for Mom to look after.

Poor Mom. This sort of thing was always happening to her. We had a penchant for collecting living things and planting them in her arms, literally or figuratively, then departing the scene while we attended to something more important. So, Mom wasn't exceptionally thrilled to get Charlotte. And she made it clear that after school, it was up to us to look after her.

So, Charlotte went to live in the chicken house for a while, where she grew on the corn we shelled and the garbage we fed her. She looked forward to our visits and became incredibly tame. She hated it when we had to leave and tried to knock down the door and follow us after feeding time. We scratched her ears, rubbed her white skin, and told her how sorry we were to leave her locked up, but it was for her own good. Of course, she didn't buy any of that nonsense; once she got big enough, she just jumped out the window and never entered a building again unless she made the decision on her own.

After Charlotte's escape, it became clear she was in charge. She slept when she pleased, ate when she pleased, walked where she pleased, dug where she pleased, and came and went as she pleased. After school, she met us at the bus and pushed us around until we stopped and scratched her back and ears before racing us to the house at top speed, gravel flying as we screamed with delight while she grunted and barked. She ran onto the porch with us, and though she'd been in the house a few times as an infant and against Mom's will, she was obliged to wait patiently until one of us came out to play with her. She raced around the yard with us, snorting and playing like any other child.

As time went by, Charlotte became immense. Pigs get really big, you know. The big boar at the Iowa State Fair can weigh over half a ton! Charlotte didn't understand the impact of her size, however. She still shoved us around and dug holes in the yard and lay in mud puddles in the driveway, but now when she shoved, she knocked us off our feet, and the holes she dug were more like canyons than anything else.

It was about this time that Charlotte developed the habit of chasing the car. We had a big Ford van, the only thing large enough to carry us all, that we took everyplace. The minute we piled in, Charlotte started squealing, as she didn't want to be left behind. At first, she just followed us tentatively down the driveway, but after a while she became more courageous and chased the van to the corner, and then eventually half a mile down the road as Mom stepped on the gas to escape her maniacal, crazed gallop. It became quite a trick to get out of the garage without the pig suddenly appearing at the corner of the house, snorting in disbelief that we dared to go off and leave her! We watched her through the back windows of the van, racing down the road, ears flapping, squealing like crazy while slowly vanishing in the distance. "Step on it, Mom! She's gaining on us!" we sang. Somehow, she always ended up back at the house, a sort of "homing pig." We were grateful she didn't follow us all the way to town; a glaring pig huffing and puffing into the shoe store would have been difficult to explain.

In August we put up a wading pool for the little kids. Iowa is terribly hot in August, so wading pools are a good thing. It didn't occur to us that the pig would think a pool was a good thing too when we filled it up that particular day. I don't know how we could have been so dumb.

The pool was full. Sandy climbed into the crystal-clear water, along with Julie. I was in charge of making certain they didn't drown, so put my shorts on and thought I would just sit in there and keep an eye on them. I climbed in as the girls splashed, practiced holding their breath, and tried to put their heads under. I spied the pig up on the drive; or more accurately, she spied me, and worse yet, she spied the water in the pool. She looked at me with her penetrating blue eyes and batted her lashes a couple of times.

Without warning, she suddenly leaped high in the air and

raced full tilt toward the pool! "Pig!!!" I screamed at the girls, for they didn't see this demonic white blur racing toward them from behind. "Pig!!!" I screamed again. The girls turned, eyes widening in horror as the pig bore down on our little pool. They screamed and thrashed about as I tried to help them to safety. Julie, five, leaped over the side, but Sandy, only three and slowed by her small size and deep water, couldn't get out fast enough, even with my help.

Charlotte flew over the side, landing smack in the middle of the pool with the force of a tidal wave. I let loose my grip on Sandy in order to shove the pig back out the way she came in, but it became quickly evident that she was not going anywhere except for where she already was, so I plucked Sandy up and jumped out. There we stood, mouths agape, while Charlotte settled herself in the cool water, just her nose sticking out. There was nothing we could do. The pig had taken our pool.

But ha-ha! The pool didn't last long! Charlotte's cloven feet poked holes in the bottom, causing it to drain after a couple of days, so she could no longer use it. Somehow there was some poetic justice there. Greedy pig.

Well, everyone reading this book knows the rule by now: all farm livestock must eventually go to the locker. From the day Charlotte arrived Dad reminded us that she'd eventually become ham and bacon.

I don't know what finally sealed her fate; perhaps it was the day Angela looked out the picture window to find herself staring at an immense pair of hams poking out of the bushes by the corner of the house.

"Look! A pig's butt!" We looked out the window to see Charlotte's disembodied butt lying motionless in the afternoon heat, with its voluptuous curves and taut skin, the rest of her sleeping carcass snoozing away under the shrubs out of sight. We imagined the scene if a big romantic boar happened to saunter by and see Charlotte's gorgeous butt in the bushes.

Apparently, the sight of Charlotte's meaty hams set Dad to think it was time to move her along to a more spiritual plane. By the time she left us she clocked in at three hundred and sixty pounds, too big to be delicious, so the meat locker docked us a few cents a pound. If they'd seen that beautiful ass warming in the sun, I think they would've paid us extra.

LORD OF THE FLIES ————

I hated my sisters' dolls, every last one of them. They had all kinds – big floppy ones, and Barbies. The dolls drank, talked, peed, cried, grew hair, and dressed to attract men. Their numbers multiplied exponentially as our number of sisters steadily increased to seven. The doll population eventually reached a critical mass that allowed them to start their own miniature village in the living room, where their hair was combed, they smoked fake cigarettes, did fashion shows, drank Martinis, and sang Kumbaya, all with the help of my sisters.

Neal and I periodically invaded, picked them off the floor, magically turned them into superheroes, and threw them with all our might to see how well they could fly, a skill the toy companies had failed to install into their otherwise full repertoires. It was very difficult to get a Barbie to fly like Superman. Her balance was off.

As difficult as they were, the Barbies made the best superheroes. They could also be strapped to chair legs as prisoners of some imaginary brute, or plunged into mud puddles, victims of violent imaginary hurricanes and floods. Poor Barbie, dragging herself through a muddy swamp only to find herself face to face with a giant cat that happened to be lurking nearby, licking its lips! At her diminutive size, the farm cats were like dinosaurs and, when forced to, would stalk, pounce, and bite Barbie. I don't think that Mattel had this sort of thing in mind when they invented Barbie, but they should have known little boys would get sick and tired of their sisters going around the house, talking imaginary girl talk with their dumb dolls, baking fake cakes, and talking to fake boyfriends. We thought it was foolish. We were *forced* to teach Barbie a lesson or two about how hard life could be in the outside world. We'd see how tough Barbie was when taken out of her prissy little element in the house!

And then of course there were the other dolls, those with stuffed cloth bodies and plastic heads and arms that wobbled around in exotic, impossible positions. These were great for throwing high in the air and landing in trees, where they would stay until a thunderstorm blew them down, soaked and messy. The girls whined and cried as they tried to get their precious little dolls out of the trees. We took great care to throw them out into the tiny, unreachable branches where they were easily snagged by their hair, and the girls couldn't climb up to get them; we enjoyed making them wait for them to fall to the ground. Of course, we offered to get them down with Dad's giant fish gig, stabbing their stuffed bodies with the tines, but the girls routinely refused that particular rescue option.

So, in this way, we tortured our sisters as much as possible. We had our boy stuff outside, our hideouts and clubs and inventions, none of which the girls were allowed to touch. We took great pains to make sure they stayed away. I don't exactly understand this tribal boy behavior, but it was a real, visceral thing.

We sometimes threatened to beat the tar out of our sisters to make them stop tagging along, or threw dirt clods or made fun of them until they cried and went back to the house. We needed privacy so we could sneak out to the creek, dam it up, and skinny-dip. We liked to build big bonfires of brush and weeds, make secret tunnels in the haymow, walk the barn beams, race our mopeds down the farm lane at breakneck speed, or work on our treehouse, a project that was never quite done. It was all secret, of course. If the girls knew what we were up to, they would always run to the house and tell Mom on us, a habit that was enormously irritating.

We had only one sister who we allowed to go with us frequently – not all the time, mind you, but much of the time – and that was Kathy. She was a tomboy and understood our tribal ways; she could join in without thinking twice about it, chucking spears and clods with masculine grace.

On the other extreme was Nancy, who not only couldn't understand our tribal needs, but couldn't bear the thought of being left behind at the house when we went off to be tribal. At the same time, if we did anything considered to be even slightly "naughty" she'd race away to tell Mom. She was the tattletale of the family. So, after letting her tag along a few times, discovering that it always resulted in a spanking and confinement to our rooms when we got back home, we nixed all future offers to her. No matter how hard she begged we wouldn't let her come along, that's all there was to it. This, of course, only served to make her mad, so she amped up her time spent chasing after us, tattling whenever she could.

"Mom, David isn't helping pick up the toys! Mom, Neal's looking at me funny! Mom, the boys won't let me play with their cars! Mom, David punched me! Mom, Neal won't stop chasing me! Mom, the boys won't let me go downstairs and roller-skate with them!" and on and on. We got so tired of it we just wanted to knock her in the head. We couldn't do *any-thing* without being tattled on. It was especially bad in the winter, because we were mostly inside and couldn't get away from her.

Well, one day Mom brought a special doll home for Nancy, a ventriloquist's dummy named Willy Talk. Get it? "Will-He-Talk." Dumb, huh? He was hideous.

Nancy had been begging for this thing for months, ever since she saw it on TV. She finally wore Mom out, so there it was in its box, with Nancy thrilled beyond measure. She carefully removed Willy from his box, taking him to her room where she played with him and got him ready for his coming out party. She taught herself how to move his arms and mouth, and practiced throwing her voice so it seemed Willy was really talking as he sat there on her lap.

This would all have been fine except for one thing; shortly after learning how to make Willy talk, Nancy decided Willy's main job was to spy on me and Neal, and tattle on us. They became our archenemies. They sat on the living room couch, mouths stern and wooden eyes glaring. Periodically Willy screamed, "Mom! The boys aren't doing what you said! They're not helping clean up the mess in here!" Mom came out of the kitchen and hollered at us to get to work. We glared at Willy and told him we were going to kill him if he didn't shut the hell up.

"Mom! The boys said 'hell!'" Willy screeched.

Mom marched in and swatted us both on the rear ends, bellering at us to stop using such language or she was going to wash our mouths out with soap. She gave us more work to do and went back to the kitchen.

"Nancy, we're gonna kill you *and* that dumb doll both if you don't shut up!"

"Mom! The boys said they're gonna kill me and Willy!" Nancy screamed. Mom spanked the daylights out of us and sent us to our bedroom. "Ha-ha!" Nancy and Willy hollered in unison.

"We have to kill that damn Willy," I told Neal. "I don't care what it takes. We have to kill him. I think we should wait until Nancy goes to town with Mom and then sneak in her room and pull his stupid head off and cut his arms and legs off." Neal agreed. There was some debate about burning him, burying him, or throwing him into the tallest tree on the farm, but in the end, we agreed on my initial plan.

We had our chance just a couple days later. Nancy went to town with Mom. We scurried into her room and opened Willy's little box. There he was. We hated him. I can still see his ugly little face to this very day — blue eyes, reddish-brown hair, freckles, pink lips, and a blue suit. Ugly, ugly, ugly.

"You stupid little jerk, Willy; you have no one to protect you now, do you? Your tattling days are over! We're gonna kill you, and there's nothing you can do about it." We jerked him out of his bed and slammed his head into the bedpost, laughing maniacally. I threw him as hard as I could against the wall. Neal picked him up, slammed him on the floor and jumped up and down on him. I picked him up by the head; Neal grabbed his legs, yanked, and popped his stupid little head off; stuffing flew all over the room.

"There, you little creep. That'll teach you a lesson you'll never forget!" We stuffed his body into his box and rolled his head under the bed.

When Nancy came home, she gaily danced into her room

to get Willy, intending, I'm sure, to put him to work spying on us again. We were sitting on the couch, waiting.

There was a scream from Nancy's room, followed by hysterical sobbing. She ran out with Willy's beheaded body, "Mom! Mom! The boys ripped Willy's head off!" she screamed.

We knew we were in trouble, but couldn't have cared less, frankly. We glared at Nancy and laughed. Mom came into the living room, took one look at Willy, and said, "What did you boys do? Did you do this? Answer me!"

"Of course, we did it," I said. "We hate that damn doll, so we killed him. All he does is tattle on us all the time. He deserved it, and if you get another one, we're gonna kill him too!"

Mom couldn't believe her ears. She grabbed us, whipped us, and dragged us to our rooms. We didn't cry or even make a sound as she waled on us, because we didn't care one bit what sort of beating we got. All we cared about was that Willy was dead; we were smug in our happiness. Mom could've spanked us nonstop for a week and we wouldn't have flinched.

As for Nancy, she sobbed for a few weeks. I don't know what she did with the remains of Willy's body or if she ever found his ridiculous head, but to this day, I don't care, and fifty years later she's still mad about it.

As our third son was about to be born, Julie and I decided to take Adam and Seth, just two and three years old, to a hospital-sponsored sibling class. We were instructed to purchase each one a realistic, life-sized infant doll which would be used to teach them how to handle a baby properly, as good brothers should.

We brought the two Cabbage Patch dolls home, and showed them to the boys. They were completely uninterested. We ex-

plained that we were going to take a class so they would learn how to have proper manners around the new baby. "Okay," they replied, then went on with their toy trucks.

At class a few days later, the boys were each presented with their doll. The instructor went around the room, talking to each child about how to be a good sibling around a baby. She went to Adam first and explained how to hold the "baby" properly. Adam did precisely what he was told, and held the "baby" perfectly, cradling its little head in the crook of his arm.

"Now, Seth, let's have you try it." She carefully placed Seth's "baby" in his arms. For a moment, Seth calmly and earnestly examined the "baby's" face, and then, with utter nonchalance, grasped the "baby's" feet and calmly slammed its head on the floor, over and over again.

"Hmmm," the teacher said. "We might have a little trouble with this one."

*A few years later, the boys were rummaging through an old box of Julie's in the storage room one day and found an old Barbie. We had never bought them dolls, except for that ill-fated sibling class, but we **did** buy them rockets so they could fire them off out in the countryside. Some of them even had tiny little GI Joes that shot out of the cone and parachuted back to earth. One day, little GI Joe landed a half mile away at the neighbors, floating down past their front porch as they sat outside for afternoon coffee time. They momentarily spit out their coffee before regaining their wits, deciding in a matter of seconds that GI Joe could only have floated in from the Coster place. A few moments later, they were at the front door where the boys were thrilled to get their GI Joe back, and incredibly amused by the story of him parachuting into the neighbor's yard.*

When the boys found the Barbie, they immediately had ideas, and before I knew it, they had her strapped to a rocket and ready to go. I found this hilarious. Barbie's breasts were a problem, though, as they were huge and would likely throw off the rocket's balance. So, the boys sort of wrapped her legs and arms around the rocket backwards so some of the weight would go to the opposite side of the rocket, then strapped her on with rubber bands. The rocket was launched and should have gone five hundred feet straight up, but instead, it managed to get about ten feet before becoming a pinwheel of fire and crashing back into the yard, Barbie's hair now melted and sticking straight out the back of her head.

Hysterics ensued, followed by days of new efforts to get Barbie to outer space. She just wasn't that good an astronaut as it turned out.

TO HELL WITH YOU KIDS!

Mom was tired of cooking. She glared at nothing in particular as she threw some more chicken into the skillet.

Day in, day out, she hovered over the stove, begging the girls to help, but all they did was whine and complain about how much work it was. No one wanted to lift a finger to assist her. Mounds of laundry to do, piles of already dried clothes on the dining room couch waiting to be folded and put away, babies to be changed and fed, but would anyone help without being asked? No! She was tired – tired about everything. She'd wanted all these kids, but she had also expected things to be different.

Dad worked hard in the fields, but he rarely helped Mom with anything around the house, and he too complained and bitched about everything. Not once did I see him pick up the vacuum cleaner, wash a window, iron a shirt, cook a meal, do a load of laundry, or change a baby. He yelled at Mom over everything; she spent too much money, bought too many groceries, didn't clean the house good enough, spent too much time at church, didn't cook enough, wanted too many things for the house, was too fat, and spent too much on gasoline. He made fun of her constantly and berated everything she did and every thought she expressed. He even made up songs about how fat she was, wandering around the house singing, "I love big fat Eleanor, I do, I do; I love big fat Eleanor, I do, I do..." thinking it was incredibly funny and somehow endearing. She wasn't particularly fat of course – all those babies had merely stretched her poor abdomen beyond belief, but he didn't care; she was supposed to have kept her svelte figure anyway; she had failed him. All he'd ever really done was destroy her self-esteem. It was his way of showing how much he loved her.

It didn't help that last Sunday, Mom's best efforts at a fantastic dinner ended in the most disastrous manner imaginable. She'd prepared a roast beef, mashed potatoes, gravy, and sweet corn in enormous tureens, all spread evenly across the table, glasses full of nutritious milk, every setting perfectly arranged. When she called "dinner's ready!" we descended on the meal like a pack of hyenas, each of us grabbing our seat, arguing about who had the best place, and grabbing for the bowls of food as fast as we could. "I had that first!" "No, I did!" "Give me those potatoes!" "No, I'm not done yet!" It was an uproar. Meanwhile, two-year-old Ev sat quietly at the end of the table, patiently and repeatedly asking for the salt, but no one would give it to her because they were too busy shoveling great gobs of food down their gullets to pay any attention to the little runt at the end. After steadily asking, and raising her voice with each request, Ev finally gave up. She stood up in her chair, nimbly stepped onto the table, and walked across it to get the salt.

Now, she had everyone's attention. Mom started hollering, Neal started laughing, and everyone backed their chairs up spontaneously, not knowing if her little feet were going to knock over glasses of milk or plop in the gravy. There were screams of delight as she somehow managed to reach the other end of the table when, unfortunately, the table legs gave way, spilling the entire dinner – plates and all – onto the floor, with Ev soaked in gravy right in the middle of the entire mess.

Nor did it help that the Sunday before that, Mom placed a huge roast in the oven before leaving for church, expecting to fix some vegetables, potatoes, and gravy when she got home for a formal, pleasant Sunday lunch with her family, only to have her plans thwarted when Sarge, our German Shepherd, swallowed the roast whole after she turned her back for a second to get the potatoes from the kitchen. At least, we think that's what happened. All we know is that the roast was on the dining room table one second and gone the next and the dog was lying under the table looking like an anaconda that had just swallowed a goat, licking his lips.

Tonight, Mom was making our favorite supper: fried chicken. She was in a foul mood, sulking and feeling sorry for herself as she worked over the stove. We loved her fried chicken and chicken gravy so much that she'd have to fix, I don't know, maybe five chickens to feed us all. We all wanted the drumsticks, but would eat any piece we could get, usually five or six per kid. That's a lot of chicken with eight kids and two adults.

She sighed heavily as she smashed the potatoes and poured flour into the skillet to make the gravy. She was mad and depressed. Stupid, thankless kids; stupid, thankless husband. Stupid dog. They're all stupid and worthless.

She slammed the first round of fried chicken onto the table, and then the second. A huge vat of mashed potatoes followed. We all began grabbing, filling our plates, chomping like lions at a fresh carcass, hollering and screaming, gulping milk, fighting, and generally acting like idiots. Mom turned back to the stove and continued to stir the gravy, looking frustrated and mad. After a minute, she turned off the burner, poured the gravy into a big tureen, and placed it on the table. After wiping her hands, she came to the table and sat down, only to find that with complete disregard for her, we'd taken and eaten every bit of chicken she'd placed on the table.

At that, she burst into tears, stood up, and blubbered, "I hate you kids! You don't give a damn what I do for you around here! You just make messes and eat up everything in sight! I cook all day and you can't even save me one little piece of chicken! *To hell with you kids! I'm never cooking another meal around here again!*"

And she never did.

From then on, I lived on ice cream and Fortified Oat Flakes and an occasional egg I fried in an inch of Crisco.

EVEN SO ────────────────

The dust from the gravel road settled lightly in the hot August air, dazzlingly white in the sun. I ran down the long driveway with all my might, scanning frantically for him. He wasn't near the end of the driveway. There was the motorcycle, lying on its side, gasoline dripping from the gas tank into the dust on the road, handlebars bent at a garish angle, the side crushed in. There was a car in the east ditch fifty yards away and a tall young woman walking up the road toward me with a little boy in tow on one side and a young girl on the other. But where was Neal?

I ran along the west side of the road, but didn't see anything. The tall grass made it difficult. I zigzagged back and forth from one ditch to the other, joined by Mom who, pregnant once again, had raced with great speed to the scene, and Angela, and soon Nancy, and then Dad, all calling: "Neal! Neal!" The air was still, though. No response. Just dust, dust, dust falling everywhere.

And then, there he was, in the east ditch, lying face down near the shoulder of the road in a lazy, relaxed sort of way, appearing, I thought, to be asleep. "Oh! He's okay!" I thought, but Mom, being quicker than I, was already at his side and lifting his face, only to suddenly look up and tell me to go back to the house – NOW. And then Dad was beside her, and the two of them looking at him, groaning, realizing he was dead, sobbing and loudly praying to God for a few seconds that it wasn't true, that He had to intervene, and then…"EVERY-ONE GET BACK TO THE HOUSE! You mustn't see this, you mustn't see…oh Johnny, his head is split open…"

I didn't want to go to the house. I wanted to stay there with my brother, but I was scared. I didn't know what was going on or what to do, but I went back, as I was told. We all did, along with the poor lady who hit him, along with her kids, and eventually along with a truck driver who had seen the whole thing in his rearview mirror and came back to see what happened. Mary Ann met me as I came in the back, screaming, "Is he dead? Is he dead?" and when I replied, "Yes," she shrieked and ran; ran as fast as she could to her room where she remained wailing for hours. To this day she remembers nothing of that morning, not even the slightest thing.

We sat in shock in the living room, making small talk with poor Mrs. Terrell, whose husband was called and soon showed up to take her and her two kids home. An ambulance came. I snuck out of the house and back to an area near the scene behind some bushes along the road, watching Mom and Dad and the volunteer ambulance crew getting Neal out of the ditch. They gently lifted his limp body out of the ditch, placed it on a narrow bed with wheels, and covered him with a sheet. They loaded him through the back doors of the ambu-lance, to be hauled to the funeral home, Mom and Dad losing their minds.

"Be careful with him, be careful with him," I thought. I suddenly had visions of Aunt Cora bouncing down the front stairs under a sheet and into the snow, then being loaded into the hearse. My mind was weeping as I watched this last memory of my brother, my eyes too shocked to produce the tears I felt inside.

Everything was a mashup in my mind after that. Mom and Dad were back at the house looking stunned, we kids were just wandering around the house. People began arriving at the house, first in a trickle and then by the dozen, bringing food and tears, hugs and empty words, not knowing what to do, so cleaning the house for us and just staying around, trying to protect us from our grief.

The funeral was slow motion. Dreamlike. Dad pleaded with the funeral director to let him see Neal one last time, but he wouldn't allow it. Too "banged up," he said. Dad stood by the casket, crying, and crying, and crying. We walked into the church, following the casket down the aisle, and took our assigned family seats. I looked only straight ahead, my lip trembling. The pastor directed us to a hymn. We opened the hymnal, and we sang: "When peace, like a river, attendeth my way, when sorrows like sea billows roll; whatever my lot, Thou hast taught me to say...*Even so, it is well with my soul.*" But I knew it wasn't well at all, and never would be. And then, turning to leave the overfilled church, and seeing so many young faces of our schoolmates and their parents, my own grief finally overcame and sank me, my tears finally flowing like a river.

The ensuing weeks were awful; Dad wailing all night in an impossible way, nonstop, until sunrise, for days and days on end. I couldn't sleep. As time went on, I prayed to God that I would never lose a child; as hard as it was for me, it was way harder for Dad. I could see that. How many times did he get in the car and fly down the road, slamming on his brakes at the mailbox to test his theory that the woman was driving too fast to stop? Fifty? A hundred? We became more frightened with each insane slamming on of the brakes, each new dust cloud hanging in the air, each wail of despair. He was so distraught we thought he'd die too, his guilt so great at having bought his beloved son that stupid motorcycle last spring that he had to place angry, sobbing blame on the rest of us, so he wouldn't have to look at his own complicity. Only Mom remained strong, bolstering her courage with the certainty that Neal was with God, that somehow God needed him worse than we did, as the preacher said. She kept her head up and her eyes clear until everyone else recovered enough to let her break down six weeks later, weeping in a way that only a mother could, knowing the pain it took to give her son life. Could it have been only thirteen years ago?

Dad had always wanted a motorcycle for himself and was always stopping in at the Honda dealer in Oskaloosa, who also happened to be the Ford dealer. He would study every bike and ask all sorts of questions, but never bought any. And then one day, he did. He bought a bike. And just as he was handed the signed papers, my sister Kathy, who was sitting and playing on the motorcycle at the far end of a row of perhaps twenty motorcycles, tipped the motorcycle over, and down went the entire row like dominoes, a bad omen if ever there was one. After writing a check for $2,500 in damages for the entire row of motorcycles, Dad finally escaped the dealership with his new motorcycle, but he was hopping mad at Kathy. When we got home, we all ran into the house to tell Mom that Dad had bought a new motorcycle and had it in the truck, and Kathy had tipped over all the motorcycles in the store. Mom was, as usual, doing dishes, and she was crying while at it. She really needed new furniture and Dad wouldn't get it for her, though she'd been talking to him about it for a year. "I hope he kills himself on it!" she said as she slammed the dishes into the sink.

I went back outside to see what Dad was going to do. I told him that Mom was really mad and was crying, hard. He shrugged and rolled the bike down a ramp and out of the truck. "Drive it!" all of us kids demanded. Dad looked at the fuel gauge, sat on the bike, and turned the key. He pulled the choke and pushed the start button. The motorcycle roared to life. He closed the choke and sat there, revving the engine, fiddling with the clutch and locating the hand and foot brakes. He hadn't read the owner's manual. He pushed the shifter down into first gear, then up to second gear. "Go, go!" we yelled as he drove up the rpms. And so, he went. He rolled the throttle and let out the clutch abruptly. The bike leapt forward with astonishing speed and popped a wheelie. In his excitement, Dad accidentally kept the throttle wide open, the bike racing off with him toward the machine shed. He had to be doing 40 mph when he threw himself off the bike just a half second before it crashed headlong into the back of the machine shed. The bike lay on the ground roaring away, the back wheel just a blur. We stared in disbelief, then ran into the house to tell Mom that Dad had just killed himself on the motorcycle. "Good!!! He deserves it!" She didn't even go out to see.

Dad eventually picked himself up, walked over to the bike, and hit the kill switch. Without a word, he righted it, rolled it back up the ramp, and took it back to the dealership. The next day he took Mom to town for that new furniture she wanted.

But then, Neal harped at Dad for the next several months

to get *him* a motorcycle. "I won't wreck it like you did," he explained. "You just didn't know how to handle it."

Eventually, Dad succumbed. He went back to Oskaloosa, and Neal picked out an orange and white Honda 175. He could not have been happier. He read the instructions, leaped on the bike, and off he went, like a pro. Within a day, he was racing it all over the farm and had created a jump area in the ditch. I wanted to ride it too, but he wouldn't let me touch it until Dad told him he had to let me ride it. He begrudgingly allowed it. I tipped it over a few times but eventually got the hang of it and became pretty good, though I was never as much of a daredevil as Neal.

That summer Neal was in trouble all the time. He kept sneaking off with the bike, eventually driving it all the way to New Sharon on the back roads and giving his friends in town rides. He came back home without anyone even knowing he had been gone, but the next day Mom ran into another mother at the store who said, "That's a really nice motorcycle you guys got for Neal." "Oh, how do you know about that?" Mom asked.

"Well, he was riding around yesterday with one of my boys." "In TOWN?" Mom sputtered. "Well, yes, in town."

Neal was too young for a permit, let alone a license. Farm kids always had minibikes and dirt bikes back then and as long as they just rode them on the farm and gravel roads nobody paid any attention to them – they didn't need a license to ride on the farm. But in town? Yes.

So, the bike key was confiscated for a week. Neal was furious that he had been caught and even more furious that the key had been taken away. The following Tuesday, August 15th, Mom got all of us up early to go register for school.

She wanted to be there by 8 a.m. Neal was supposed to get his key back that morning, and he wanted it back before we left. He insisted until Mom gave it to him, and she told him to wait until we got back from town to ride. He did not. He raced out to the garage, started the bike, and raced down the driveway.

It turned out we had the wrong day. School registration was on Thursday, not Tuesday.

I heard the bike roar to life and saw Neal heading out. The window was open, and I started to yell at him to turn around, but he zoomed past the window so fast he couldn't have heard me. Kathy was watching him out the dining room window when the car hit him. We all heard it; it was loud. She saw his body fly through the air and down the road. "A police car hit Neal!" she screamed. "What?!" We all ran for the front door, Mom going out the back, as it was closer to her. Down the drive we raced. I couldn't figure out why a police car would have been out there, let alone hitting my brother on his motorcycle. Well, of course it wasn't a police car. We came upon the scene. Within an hour, answers as to what happened became clear. Neal was being unruly and impetuous. As he raced the bike down the driveway, a truck drove past, throwing up a cloud of dust. A car was coming from the other direction and drove into the dust cloud. Neal, enveloped in a dust cloud, drove right out into the car's path, likely never even seeing it. Bang! He went flying through the air, end over end, landing in the east ditch, only to have his head run over by the front right tire of the car as it careened into the ditch. That's what happened.

I went off to eighth grade a couple weeks later, as if nothing happened, wearing Neal's favorite shirt. I had gone through all of his clothes and started wearing them. People looked at me and whispered. Some were startled to see me; they'd heard it was me who was dead. No one knew what to say, or when to say it. The atmosphere was strained. I tried not to cry at school and just focused on my books. The days were hot and unbearably long and home seemed far away.

The bus dropped us off every afternoon at the driveway. Each time, I looked at the spot where Neal died; I couldn't help it. I trudged to the house, hoping for some peace, but there was no peace in our house anymore.

The world had shifted.

Thirty-three years later, a pleasant elderly gentleman from New Sharon toddled into my office with his wife to talk to me about a surgical problem. I knew him and his wife a little. They were the same age as Mom.

We chatted a bit, me catching up on news from "down home." He asked about Mom and talked about the farm a bit and asked about my brothers and sisters.

"I'll never forget about your brother," he said after a bit. "I was there you know." He looked tearful. "You were?" I said, surprised.

"Yes," he replied, now with true tears running down his face. "It's my fault he's dead." "What?" I asked incredulously. "What are you talking about? Neal drove out in front of a car. It was no one's fault but his own."

"No. It was my fault," he began again. "I was driving a big gravel truck past your house that day, going north. I saw Neal coming down the driveway on his motorcycle. It was a really hot, dry day, and my truck was throwing up a lot of dust on the gravel road. I went past your driveway and met a car go-

ing south. I could still see Neal coming down the driveway for a second in the side mirror, but then he vanished from sight in the dust from my truck, and then I saw a huge cloud of dust and heard a big bang when that poor woman hit him. The dust from my truck kept him from seeing that car, and kept her from seeing him. I turned around and went back, but there was nothing I could do."

He was really crying now. "For heaven's sake," I said gently, grabbing his arm. "You're the man who came to the house right after the accident. It wasn't your fault. Neal knew to stop and look before leaving the driveway. He just didn't do it that morning. He was a reckless and foolish boy sometimes, and that's why he's gone. You have to stop blaming yourself. It's been thirty-three years. You deserve some peace. Bad things just happen sometimes. I'm so sorry you've suffered with this all this time. Please, it wasn't your fault."

He blubbered a little more while I sat quietly, thinking. I remembered him sitting on our couch. The poor guy; he was a strapping man of forty when that happened. Now he was a little fragile guy of seventy-three with arthritis and a bad back. How much of his fragile health is due to carrying this terrible burden around all these years, I wondered.

"You have to let it go now," I told him.

Now it's forty-one years later. The living room is dark, and I'm lying on the couch, alone, in the middle of the night. I am swallowed up in grief. My youngest son, Sam, has just been diagnosed with a horrible type of Stage 4 lymphoma.

"He almost certainly won't survive; there is less than a seven percent chance. He could be gone within days," the oncologist had told me privately.

And then, I'm remembering that night on the living room couch decades ago, when at twelve, while listening to Dad wail, I prayed to God I would never lose a child, and then my own wailing begins, and I sink so deep into a black abyss I think I will never come out.

PART TWO

TILTING AT WINDMILLS ———————

We all have many crosses to bear in our youth. Mine was Dad's windmill project. He attacked it with a vengeance a few months after Neal died, I guess because he would have gone insane without something to preoccupy him twenty-four hours a day. My own grief was left to heal quietly on its own the best it could.

A lack of education beyond high school didn't stop Dad from having big ideas. He had done some pretty amazing things with farm equipment and was frequently featured in the newspaper for his progressive ideas for farming and inventing new ways to use big equipment. It was a source of great pride for him. He always described his work as "play," because he loved it so much. He couldn't imagine being anything but a farmer.

During the '70s, there was a serious energy crisis, enough so to get Dad thinking he had to reduce energy costs at home. He pondered and doodled, he read, and talked to himself and local engineering types day in and day out, and eventually came up with an idea.

Wind as a source for energy was not a new idea; in fact, there were many well-trained engineers successfully working on wind energy around the country already, but having studied their plans, Dad determined he was eminently more qualified to make the perfect windmill to generate electricity.

Thus, my teenage years were ruined.

I was thirteen when it began. Dad was still constantly working on it twenty-five years later, a monument to his never-ending grief over the loss of his beloved son.

It started with just a few plans scribbled on papers, then long sessions with Gary Kelderman in Oskaloosa, who owned a machine shop, and visits to Carter's Steel, the lumber yard, Bernstein's junkyard, and all sorts of out-of-the-way places where parts could be bought or scavenged for next to nothing. He plotted and schemed on the tower and blade design, the type of generator to attach to the semi-tractor axle he'd decided to use for the hub, the pad design, and energy storage. We spent an entire year building a small model of his dream machine on a regular old windmill tower planted out back, anchored to the house and a liquid propane tank with guy wires.

Day in and day out we worked; in sun, rain, hail, and snow, from sunup to well after sundown. I hated it so much I wanted to put my eyes out. Ten o'clock at night, twenty below zero, my homework not done, or 115 degrees in the shade and heat stroke warnings out, it didn't matter. I held steel parts while he drilled and torched and filed and hammered.

When the "model" didn't quite work, I timidly suggested perhaps he should just give up and buy one already designed by the appropriate engineers. He considered my opinion for a billionth of a second, then immediately dove into his plans for the big one, the one that would not only provide electricity for the farm, but the entire state as well. He'd eliminate his energy bills and sell the extra electricity back to the power company at a huge profit. We'd be millionaires, and famous ones at that.

His design was simple. A tower sixty feet tall made of solid steel pipe, three feet in diameter, bolted to a cement pad buried six feet in the ground, held stable by six huge steel pipes branching out in all directions like an octopus, attached both to the cement and the center of the tower, some thirty feet up where the catwalk would be located. A platform would be attached to the very top, centered on a semi-axle hub so it could rotate with any change in wind direction. Electrical wires would run into the tower from a generator sitting on the platform, and the generator would be attached to yet another semi-axle hub to which the forty-foot wheel would be attached. The "wheel" would mimic the design of the regular little windmills that dotted the landscape at the time, with their little blades spaced regularly around the perimeter.

We needed big batteries to store the electricity too. Big four-hundred-pound batteries from the telephone company, as a matter of fact. A couple hundred of them should do, housed in the garage.

When not in school, I went with Dad to get the stuff for the windmill. By the time I was sixteen, the project was finally coming together, and Dad was really getting wound up. Success was imminent. We dug the hole, poured the cement, put up the tower, attached the generator, applied the hub, and installed the batteries. We were almost ready. Only the wheel attachment remained.

Dad decided on a complex reinforcement strategy to support the blade arms, welding re-rod at multiple points between the triple-pipe design that would support each blade. It was my job to hold the re-rod in position as he welded it, a task that took several weeks.

Not having an extra welding helmet, I was supposed to keep my eyes closed in order to keep the bright light of the welder from burning my retinas out while Dad welded merrily away. One day while thus blinded, a spark flew up and landed on the faux fur lining of my denim jacket, catching it on fire. I stood there, burning along, completely unaware of my predicament. I may even have been humming a tune to dispel my boredom, when all at once Dad started hitting and punching me in the belly and chest like crazy, knocking me off my feet. I dutifully kept my eyes closed as instructed while he continued to beat me, though yelping now and then. I finally opened my eyes to chew him out for this unprovoked assault, only to find the front of my coat burned off – a close call I could have done without. I thanked him for beating me up to put out the fire, repositioned my grip, closed my eyes, and got back to work.

But that incident was nothing. We kids were assigned to hook up the two-hundred batteries in the garage in parallel. Steel connectors had to be bolted from one battery terminal to the next, connecting them all. There were so many it required child labor to finish the task, so Kathy and Julie were nabbed to help with the project, an all-day affair. We were warned NOT to accidentally touch any wrenches or metal objects between the wrong terminals or there would be a big explosion. We painstakingly attached the bars, one by one, until all the rows of batteries were hooked together.

I climbed to the top row to attach the last terminals together. Kathy was still working down below, finishing up the bottom two rows. All the batteries were partially juiced up – they came that way from the phone company. Finished, I jumped from the top cross arm onto the cement below, landing in a shower of sparks, explosions, flying molten lead, and smoke galore. I could see nothing – the brightness of the melting terminals temporarily blinded me. All I could think was that Kathy must have accidentally touched her wrench across the terminals, killing us all in one fell swoop. I crouched on the cement for what seemed an eternity. The explosions stopped and the smoke slowly cleared. I looked up, surprised to be alive. I scrambled out of the wreckage, looking for Kath, and found her standing beside the batteries, looking bewildered.

"What did you do?" I asked. "What did YOU do?" she replied. "What did you guys do?" Dad screamed.

Hell, I didn't know what happened. I thought Kath did it, she thought I did it, and Dad thought we somehow both did it. In a few minutes, we determined that I had done it when I jumped from the top, my foot catching a big cable that swung around and shorted out on the metal frame of the battery stands, using up the voltage in the top two rows of batteries in a matter of seconds. The only thing that saved me was landing safely on my feet on the cement without touching anything metal around me; Kathy just happened to step back at the same instant, a stroke of luck. Julie, not enjoying the work, had thankfully wandered off several minutes before to do something else.

We moved on as though nothing had happened. By this time, the gigantic wheel was completed but lay helplessly on the ground. The generator was painfully put in place on the top of the tower with an old crane – during a thunderstorm. All was ready.

The day of the wheel-raising began bright and clear, with light winds from the north. I was rousted out of bed early so we could get the wheel attached before the winds rose and caught the windmill's enormous blades. It was now October, and cold.

I shivered into my stupid insulated rubber boots and trudged out the door, wishing I was anyplace but there. What other teenage boy in the country was doing such a ridiculous thing on an otherwise perfectly good Saturday morning? Dad started the crane truck, an old thing we just happened to have handy around the house to "do stuff" with, and I hooked the log chains onto the hub of the wheel. Of course, I didn't do it properly, so Dad had to climb off the crane and sarcastically explain why I was a complete retard and how ANYBODY with any brains at all ought to know how to hook a log chain onto the hub of a giant windmill. I hated that piece-of-crap windmill like nothing else at that point.

Dad climbed back onto the crane and began lifting the wheel. The damned thing was heavy, though, a lot heavier than anyone realized. Halfway up the tower, the wheel suddenly tipped the crane off the ground, with the boom snapping in half and the whole mess crashing down on top of the chicken house, partially crushing it. Dad stood there in disbelief, but for only a moment. "Well, don't just stand there David! Unhook the log chain! We've got work to do!" he hollered.

A month later, the wheel was repaired and a new plan was nicely in place. A huge crane from town rolled onto the driveway promptly at eight o'clock and without much ado easily lifted the wheel into place sixty feet up, where I stood precariously perched on the edge of the small platform. It was my job, as the monkey in the family, to firmly apply the nuts to the bolts so the damned-fool thing would stay on the hub for the foreseeable future. I hung over the side trying to thread the nuts with my cold, numb, and barely moveable fingers. Somehow, I managed to get it all lined up and positioned, and then Dad climbed up and finished the job. He never quite trusted me.

It was a scary sight, this giant windmill. The tower sixty feet high, the wheel forty feet in diameter with nine enormous aluminum sails attached to steel-reinforced pipe reaching up to a final height of eighty feet; I mean, it was gigantic. And Dad couldn't wait to turn it on. Everyone came out to watch.

Now, Dad hadn't bothered to actually calculate the surface area necessary to provide adequate torque and horsepower to create the necessary electricity to supply the farm's needs. So, having been designed like an overgrown standard farm windmill, it had enough surface area to sail the Titanic with no engines, if you know what I mean. There was only the slightest breeze, but once the brake was released it took off like it had places to go – and we ran like hell to get out of the way. The wind picked up slightly as we watched from a safe distance of an eighth-mile, and the windmill began proving its power. The earth began to vibrate as the tower trembled on its solid cement foundation. The whir of the blades could be heard for a half-mile; the tips must have been flying at the speed of light. I stood in awe, scared out of my wits.

About then, Dad hollered at me to climb the tower and apply the brake to stop the thing. I wasn't sure I'd heard properly. "What?" I said.

"Climb up there and pull the brake! It can't be that hard. Just wait until the blades are away from the top of the ladder at the catwalk and climb up! Simple!"

I was dumbfounded. "Do what?" I said again, thinking about the blades flying two feet above the catwalk at the speed of light. What if there was a sudden change in wind direction? "I'll be cut to ribbons!" I hollered back. "I am NOT going up there! YOU go if you think it's so damned easy!"

He looked at me with disgust. Turning, he walked the distance to the tower. We all held our breath. The wheel was yawing this way and that, the earth vibrating; Dad started up the main ladder to the catwalk. Half way up, he just stood there, staring into the thing he'd created. There was no stopping it. It was an uncontrollable monster that could kill us all. Aggravated, he backed slowly down the ladder.

We all walked to the relative safety of the house – all but Dad, that is – where we spied on the monster through the dining room window, watching its wildly waving arms. Periodically it slowed a little and Dad thought he might stop it, so he kept hanging around it to get his chance. But every time there was a momentary lull, it caught another breeze and took off again. We kids played Parcheesi in the dining room and ignored it, but we all knew it was still there. Occasionally the house vibrated a little and we cowered around the table wondering when one of the arms would fly off and come crashing through the dining room ceiling. Dad came in and kept telling us it had to stop eventually, but we all knew better. The wind doesn't stop very often in Iowa in the winter.

After a quiet and fearful lunch, I went to the high school for a rare Saturday afternoon basketball practice. I drove home hesitantly afterward, hoping against hope that something had changed, but no such luck. I parked the car a good distance away from the groaning thing and worked my way to the front door, watching cautiously out the corner of my eye lest the beast should suddenly release an arm and cut me in two. It was windier than ever, and I couldn't imagine how much more it could take.

About five in the afternoon, as we sat at the dining room table playing cards, there was a powerful "crack." We reached the window just in time to see one of the enormous blades flying in a great arc over the field. It landed with a thud, piercing three feet into the frozen earth. The sudden shock of losing an arm sent the monster into a wild, uncontrolled flailing as it lost its balance. With one last powerful groan, it then went completely crazy and wrapped its remaining arms around the tower. All was silent. The ground stopped shaking, the chandelier stopped swinging, and we stood there staring at it in the twilight.

Dad looked for a minute. "Hmm. I know JUST how to fix it! David! Come on!"

But there were other things to do as well while the windmill was being restored, as in attending to all the requests from surrounding towns for crane work. Dad had the old crane repaired so we could continue as usual with erecting buildings, cutting down trees, lifting farm machines and grain bins, and generally just picking things up from great heights whenever anyone needed it. Dad bought that crane partway through the windmill project. It was sort of a truck, with a boom on the trailer – very old-fashioned looking. The controls were behind the cab, so one person had to stand there on a little platform and operate the boom up, down, in, out, and side-to-side as needed for the job. There was also a cable with a hook and other attachments to help with whatever task might come up. The crane tended to break down fairly frequently. Dad, of course, decided that I had to be a crane operator. He also wanted me to be the guy in the crane bucket with a chainsaw to top trees, trim them, or remove them entirely, and some of these trees were gigantic. It's not an easy task to manhandle a chainsaw while cabled into a tiny fiberglass bucket, and Dad didn't make it any easier with his erratic maneuvers with the crane boom. He would ram me right through a bunch of branches without warning or swing me side to side without giving me a heads-up. I learned to dive down into the bucket, if necessary, until the boom stopped jerking around. During my teenage years, I became quite savvy with a chainsaw. But I always accused Dad of trying to kill me everytime I went up in the boom.

One day we were summoned by the City of Oskaloosa to trim and/or remove a bunch of large trees surrounding an old dilapidated house. We were told there was an old man who lived in there in a pile of cardboard boxes, crazy as a loon, who did NOT want any of his overgrown property to be touched by anyone. We were assured that the proper legal documents had been filed to address the "public nuisance" status of his house and lot, and that the police would be readily available just in case of any trouble.

We pulled up and set up the crane to get started. At first, all was status quo, but then the old man came out, hollering and swearing and having a conniption fit. As the guy ran around and around the crane, Dad just laughed, flicking the boom here and there so I could drop the offending limbs to the overgrown weed patch below. We finished a couple smaller trees, and then moved on to the biggest one. As Dad pushed me through that tree, the boom suddenly began yawing back and forth in an extreme manner. I turned around and looked down, yelling at Dad to "stop trying to kill me," when I realized the problem. The lunatic now had a gun and was threatening first to shoot Dad, and then shoot me. He swung the gun around toward Dad, then swung it back up toward me, finally firing a round as I dropped down into the bucket to protect myself as best I could. There was a lot of yelling and continued swinging of the boom as Dad tried to stay out of aim while keeping me swinging around enough to make it hard for the dude to shoot me. Finally, there were sirens and six police cars, and the man was wrestled to the ground and taken off in handcuffs, Dad laughing his head off at the whole scene. They kept him in jail until we were done, then let him go back home, as he was normally harmless.

A week later we were called to a farmhouse up the road to remove the top fifty feet of a gigantic silver maple tree. I took the big saw up with me, as the trunk, even at that height, was alarmingly thick. I confirmed the cut location with hand signals from Dad and then began sawing. Partway through, a whole bunch of water started pouring out of the cut, something I had never seen happen before. I shrugged and kept going. I knew that silver maples tended to be hollow. There was an open snag at the top of the tree, and I figured the hollow center must have filled with rainwater.

I continued sawing merrily away until the entire top fifty feet of the tree suddenly gave way and flew to the ground below, whereupon, immediately, the air around the crane was absolutely filled with honey bees. The "water" in the tree was not water, it was honey, and this must have been the biggest hive of honeybees in the world, and they were all out and furious and looking for anything that moved.

Being still sixty feet up, I was perfectly safe, in a way. The bees were all down there. But I was also a sitting duck. If they decided to come up. I had no place to escape; I was just hanging there in mid-air with no place to go. Meanwhile, Dad was now getting stung repeatedly. He yelled at the top of his lungs that he was bringing me down fast. I ducked into the bucket and unhooked my tether so I could make a quick escape once I was on the ground. He dropped me so fast I was transiently weightless, and then, boom, I was on the ground. I threw the chainsaw over the side and leaped out into the thickest swarm of bees I had ever seen. Dad jumped off the control bridge of the truck at the same time and we ran like hell for the tall corn, the obvious place to hide. But no, the bees followed us. They were in my hair and getting into my shirt and into Dad's overalls. We were not safe there, so we ran out of the corn and toward the farmhouse, the bees after us in high gear. We arrived at the front door and just ran in full tilt, swatting bees left and right, with me ripping my shirt off as fast as I could.

It took me a minute to realize that we were being watched by the old farm couple who, upon our entrance, were sitting right in front of us on their living room couch, coffee cups in hand. "Bees! Bees!" I yelled as I pulled my pants off and scraped the bees off my legs and underwear. The poor couple was so startled they couldn't even talk! And some of the bees were now loose in the house, not a typical situation for morning coffee. I threw my pants back on and asked them for a fly swatter. I ran around the living room finishing off the attacking hoard. Meanwhile, Dad was directed to an adjacent mudroom to shake out his overalls. Then, we just had to stay awkwardly in the house for an hour, making small talk and waiting for the bees to calm down.

The crane was still running and needed to be shut off. We made one attempt, but we couldn't get anywhere near it with ten billion enraged bees surrounding it. Dad, as always, knew exactly what to do. He decided he was just going to let the crane sit there all day until it ran out of gas. We would wait two days and then come back and get it and clean up the tree limbs. He asked to use the phone at the farmhouse and called Mom to come and get us. We ran to the car, escaping with our lives and with a hilarious story to tell.

⤳

"Do you think we should call Dr. Jadali for help?" Dr. Swegle asked me as I deftly stuffed my left index finger into the space between the aorta and vena cava, at once stopping the torrent of blood filling the abdomen. "Nope. I know just how to fix it, Swegle. I'm leaving my finger in the hole; you cut over here and rotate the spleen and colon and pancreas over so we can get above it and see what we're doing; I can use my right hand to help."

In two minutes, the maneuver was done, and I could see where the clamp needed to go. I deftly swept a finger behind the vessels. "Here, grab an angled vascular clamp and slide it around, Jim. I made a tunnel already with my finger. Quick, just right there. That's it, perfect! Clamp the bitch!"

"Now, I'll compress below and use the suction as a retractor and sucker, and you load up that stitch and sew like hell!"

The next day on rounds, Dr. Jadali, or "Jad" as we called him, was incredulous. "You did what? You had a guy with a bullet through his liver, stomach, duodenum, vena cava, and aorta and you FIXED IT BY YOURSELVES?"

"Well, yes," I replied. "Isn't that what we're supposed to do? Fix things?"

"Well, have you EVER done that sort of repair before???"

"No, but we've read about all these types of things, and

frankly, we didn't think it was that hard. Decisions had to be made. Obviously, we would have called you if we truly needed you, Jad, but we were just too busy solving the problem to interrupt our work for a phone call. Besides, we figured you needed your sleep at two in the morning. And look at the guy, he's just fine. See?"

And he WAS just fine. In fact, he was sitting up in bed, glaring at the nurses, and yelling at them to bring him some goddamned fucking breakfast before he ripped their heads off. Of course, being the sociopathic drug dealer he was, he'd already yanked out his endotracheal tube and IV's and put his dirty clothes back on and was ready to leave the hospital.

"Now, Mr. Jones," I said. "You really should get some rest and settle down! That bullet went through some critical things in there and you have one hell of a whack on your belly. You can't just jump out of bed and go home. You'll die, you nitwit."

"Really?" he barked. "Watch this."

And he got out of bed, shoeless, and just walked right out the door, down the hall, and out the exit before anyone could do a thing about it.

TOOL TIME ————————————

One particularly hot, steamy, August day, the detasslers happened to come by. Detasslers are a breed of rowdy teenage kids who don't much exist anymore, as machines have taken their jobs almost entirely, but in 1975 they were a big motley crew of teenage boys and girls dressed in cutoffs and tank tops whose job it was to remove the tassels from the female corn plants in the seed corn fields. It was hard, hot, sweaty summer work, but it was relatively lucrative compared to other things, so many town kids did it, as well as country kids.

Early in the morning, one of the girls on the crew told the foreman she was sick. She was sent to the bus, where she sat spying on my lean, muscular, fifteen-year-old body as I worked on the stupid windmill. I always worked in nothing but jeans and work boots in the summer, my body golden from the sun and my long '70s hair a platinum sheen, a farmboy look that many town girls found downright irresistible, as did the one on the bus.

All at once, she was beside me, her shadow cast across my blond head, blocking out the sun. I looked up. Her lustrous deep red hair hung limply, curling around and caressing her huge breasts as she sidled up to the equipment I was working on. "Hi," she said languidly, eyes half-closed. "I saw you working over here, and thought, well, I'll just come over." I grunted in response and turned back to my work, my guard up. Out of the corner of my eye, I saw her studying me seductively as I struggled to line up two bolt holes with a punch – an eight-inch solid-steel tool used specifically for that task. She studied the punch. "You know," she stated, as she admired the length and girth of my tool, "I really like long…hard…things." Clearly, the sight of the punch, its full eight-inch, rock-hard steel shaft glinting in the sun, had given her some ideas. "How old are you?" I asked. "Fourteen," she purred. "I look old for my age." I suddenly felt like a fly caught in a web, the web of a big, hungry, giant-breasted, redheaded spider who would consider my release if I gave her what she wanted. And what she wanted was my tool.

I knew the other boys in my class would have joined her back on the bus as quick as a wink, bragging when school started about how they'd "got some" from this hot little red-headed chick. It crossed my mind that maybe this was exactly the opportunity I needed to prove that I could do it with a girl. But having never done it, I didn't know how to go about it for sure, and all I felt was a deep, gripping fear in the pit of my stomach. So, I did what any good kid would do in such a situation; I put down my tools and said, "Really? That's nice," and ran for the house as fast as I could, where I promptly told Mom on her.

I wish I'd just handed her that eight-inch punch and said, "Here ya go, honey. Have fun!" before I ran away, but for all I know she may have taken it to the bus anyway.

Mom, for her part, kept me safely protected in the house until the detasslers left, the redheaded sex fiend waving gaily at me from the bus, empty-handed, as she passed by the dining room window where I stood watching.

I must admit I had very little interest in the budding

womanhood around me at school. The other boys were keenly interested in so-and-so's breasts, calves, curving hips, and pouty lips; instead, I had a healthy interest in the bulge in Mark Bailey's ever-so-tight blue jeans. It wasn't a new development, of course, with my erotic memory going all the way back to those two handsome morticians who picked up Aunt Cora, but by the time I reached tenth grade, I began to wonder if something was wrong with me. I couldn't understand why Ronnie and Tony were getting so lathered up about Polly or Jill's new fantastic bodies – I absolutely didn't get it. I could watch those girls all day long and it just didn't seem to have the same effect. Watching the other boys however, with their newly powerful chests and thighs, well, that was another story altogether.

The locker room became a sort of torture chamber. "Keep your eyes straight ahead, no looking around," I'd say to myself as I stripped down. "Just hurry up and shower, get dressed, and get out of here," became my personal mantra, muttered repeatedly under my breath as I stood under the shower. Everyone else laughed, talked, slid naked on the shower room floor, snapped their towels on bare asses, and grabbed at each other's dicks and balls while making derogatory or complimentary comments about them. Sometimes they even pretended to hump each other as a hilarious joke, the victim pretending to be horrified and yelling, "Get off of me, you stupid homo!" Not everyone participated in the sex play; some merely watched these antics with amusement. The topic of conversation during this play was, of course, primarily girls and sex; none of them were aroused to the point of more than a semi-hard-on by this horsing around. The ironic juxtaposition of the homoeroticism between these straight jocks who were always screaming "fag" at the non-jock boys apparently went completely over their heads. It was all very confusing. What I saw as intensely erotic, they saw as slapstick comedy. Something was definitely wrong with me.

To add to my confusion was the fact that ever since fifth grade, the boys in the class had maintained a healthy interest in each other's genitals, inspecting and playing with them all the time. Sleepovers often reportedly turned into mutual masturbation sessions, and on one occasion, an entire crowd of seventh-graders tore holes in all the stuffed animals in their host's house so they could all practice fucking them. Or so I heard. I don't know how they explained away the raped teddy bears the next day to the parents. I myself had a couple of more mundane erotic skirmishes on stayovers with single individuals who wanted to sample what it must be like to be naked with another human being, but it never reached the level of what I heard the football players were up to with their circle jerks and "contests" (a game where everyone jacks off to see who "cums" quickest).

Meanwhile, my ever-so-well-meaning fundamentalist church pastors regularly demeaned gay men and women from the pulpit, declaring them monsters of indescribable wickedness – filthy perverts who preyed upon animals (no mention of teddy bears) and children (no mention of all the sex abuse of children committed by hetero men) to fulfill their hideous sexual desires. They were abominations who recruited young men and women into the wickedness of their ways at every opportunity (no mention of sexual horseplay in the showers), men who "lay with men" (whatever that meant, with no mention of the circle jerks and masturbation competitions by the hetero boys) and women filled with unnatural desires who could never reproduce as ordained by God. Their sexual depravity led to madness. Homosexuals were the archetype of evil, the one and only thing that could single-handedly destroy our society as we knew it, ruin families, and ultimately destroy the opportunity for all good Christians to have a normal life. They would all burn in hell, and they deserved it. They should all be stoned to death.

And that was just from the Sunday morning and Sunday evening church pulpit. Sunday school was another place to defame sex, sexual thoughts, and homosexuals.

"Masturbation is evil! God will destroy those who spill their seed upon the ground! It says so right here in the Bible!"

We boys all looked at each other. We all knew teenage boys masturbated all the time. We still appeared to be healthy – maybe it was a slow destruction of some sort we didn't know about yet. Or maybe if you just didn't cum "on the ground" you were fine. Stomach, face, headboard, socks, pillows, bathtub – all allowed. Just don't let it hit the ground.

"If you even THINK about having sex with a woman, it's the same as doing it! You may as well rape her; it's the same thing in God's eyes! Thinking it is the SAME as DOING it! Do you understand? You must abstain from all appearance of evil! You will go to hell!"

And in the newspapers:

"Homosexual Murdered after Making Pass at Man – Charges Dropped."

"Homosexual Bludgeoned to Death – No Charges to be Filed."

"Homosexuals Charged with Sodomy – Will Get Twenty Years."

"Is Homosexuality a Mental Illness? – Big Battle between the Church and the Medical Establishment."

And in the school halls:

"You fag!"

"You can't wear a yellow shirt on Thursday! It's queer day! If you wear yellow, you're a queer!"

"Hey, butt-fucker! Yeah, you! You're a fag!"

And on the athletic fields:

"What sort of catch was that, little girl? Grow some balls! Only a queer would catch like that!"

What, really, was a "homosexual?" Was it just about the sex, or was there something else wrong with them too? Were they demented? Were they really as awful as the church said they were? How did one know whether or not he was a homosexual? How did you become one? Could you be one and not really know it?

It was clearly a bad idea to be a homo; why did they choose to live a life that placed them at such risk for arrest, murder, beatings, and an eternity in hell? Their families hated them, they couldn't have kids, and they turned into raving lunatics after a while. So, why would anyone choose such a stupid path? Plus, they were always going to jail! Straight people kept throwing them in there. It was against the law to even EXIST as a homosexual!

The other boys eventually stopped their homo sex play by senior year and totally switched over to girls. It was, I reasoned, probably just a phase we all went through, one we didn't talk about. Maybe the other boys felt the same way I did but were just better at not showing it. It would go away. It had to, after all. We were all the same, and I was a really good, normal kid.

But I was left with a nagging doubt about it. I never asked any of my male classmates about how they actually felt while in the throes of their same-sex play, but I somehow knew that if I were dumb enough to ask them, it might be the last thing I ever said.

I dated a few girls as I got older, but I was mostly just the guy who was friends with every girl in the class. I got used to rationalizing, ignoring, and burying the stream of homoerotic fantasies going through my head, the only type I ever had, by immersing myself in school and working steadily on the farm, then focusing on college and medical school. I never talked about it with anyone.

I married at twenty-one, a woman I loved, my date for my senior prom. Julie and I had a perfect life together for seventeen years — health, happiness, three wonderful sons, professional success, and close friendship. How was I to know it couldn't last?

∽

I didn't know how I got home. All I knew was that I had to get my shit together and be done with this utter stupidity. How fucking stupid could I be! What the hell was wrong with me! I stood in the over-sized walk-in closet of our brand-new home, gathering my wits about me, and began taking off my suit to change into something more comfortable. I hoped Julie would not be able to see how puffy my face was from sobbing for four hours nonstop all the way from Chicago. If she asked, I would just say I seemed to have some allergies, I decided. What nonsense to be thirty-seven and dealing with such fucking goddamned stupidity. What was WRONG with me? Why was this happening?

For a year, I had been spiraling into a depression, for no reason. My practice was going great, I worked in a great hospital with great people, my partners were fantastic, my patients loved me, my work was challenging and fruitful, my boys were thriving, Julie was happy, we were happy together, we lived on a beautiful acreage and had just moved into a wonderful house that had taken an entire year to build. I had my gardening and landscaping hobbies, my birds, my prairie restoration and wildlife work; I was in good shape and felt physically fine, but something was terribly, terribly wrong emotionally, and I couldn't get a handle on it. Frequently, Julie had asked over the previous year what was wrong, but I could never articulate a response. The answer was too deep for me to grasp and look at clearly. I just wouldn't – and couldn't – seek it out. I didn't want to know.

I had been working out like a maniac to soothe my increasingly agitated psyche, so by August, 1997, when it all came to a head, I was a very slender 155 pounds, remarkably fit, and, for once in my life, I thought, even handsome. I liked how I looked in the mirror, even if I didn't like the storm in my head and how I felt every day. On one particular day that August, I ran ten miles – a record for me – and perhaps that is what finally caused me to snap, running down the hill toward the Krumm Prairie Preserve for my last mile, where I suddenly, and for no apparent reason, just stopped running. I was standing in the middle of the gravel road. Locusts were singing. It was hot. My hips hurt from the run. I looked up into an absolutely cloudless sky, and said out loud, with no forethought, "I'm gay. That's what's wrong. That's what's always been wrong." And I just kept standing there, staring into that blue, blue sky, breathing hard and listening to my heart pound, and feeling the sweat running down my back. I stood there like a statue for fifteen minutes, planted squarely in the middle of the road.

I continued on, then, one foot in front of the other, down the hill and back up again, as awareness washed over me. I had been running from myself all summer, running from the fact of my gayness, physically acting out my own emotional reaction to my subconscious self that could no longer be held at bay. It suddenly all became so goddamned clear, and I began to feel momentarily better. But by the time I was running up the drive to my beautiful place, my wife, and my kids – the family that mattered to me most of all – I was physically ill.

Later that month, I went to Chicago for a week-long surgery conference. I went to the gym at the hotel there one day to work out, where I saw, coming out of the swimming pool, a man whose look completely destroyed me, and for the first time in my life I was overpowered with desire that could no longer be ignored – just from looking at him from a distance. I almost collapsed. I looked away. "Who is that man?" I asked the desk clerk, knowing that she likely had no idea. "Oh, he's one of our therapists – a great guy." I went on and did my workout but didn't look back at him. I knew I was in trouble. I had not counted on this. In fact, I had decided over the past two weeks that it didn't matter that I was gay; I had managed just fine all these years and I had responsibilities and a wife and kids and a life and a profession and there was no room for being gay in that equation. I had boxed it in all this time, and it would just have to stay boxed in. I was mentally and emotionally tough and had dealt with much worse things in my life, I thought, and I would control this just like I had controlled and worked out those other things through the years. I had a lot of life scars and had done a lot of self-healing. This would be the same.

The next day I went down to the gym for a massage, only to discover that my scheduled therapist was ill and would not be able to do it. "You will have Mark instead," the clerk chirped happily. "He's the guy you asked about yesterday."

And thus, the storm began that led me into our walk-in closet one afternoon the following January. I had fallen in love with Mark so fast it made my head swim. I couldn't help it. A dam had burst, and I had drowned. And after four months of desperate love and terror, I had canceled my clinic and driven all the way to Chicago to see him for the last time and tell him goodbye forever, having once again decided that my obligations to the world I had created superseded whatever it was that I needed so badly from Mark. Julie had been worried sick about me and had, about three weeks earlier, "accidentally" happened upon a journal entry in my desk, exposing my agony. She had already suspected that it was my sexuality that was causing my depression, but the journal entry had then proven it, and she had been turning this information over and over in her mind for those three weeks, wondering what in the world she should do, and how to bring it up. She was scared to death for my safety as she watched me becoming sadder and sadder and thinner and thinner. She had given me several opportunities to open up to her, but each time I turned away, not being ready to talk about something I hadn't yet figured out how to deal with myself. So, she found Mark's number and called him that day, January 2nd, 1998, and Mark told her the truth about what was going on. In fact, she had already talked to him before I even arrived in Chicago, but he said not a word to me about it.

I was so grief-stricken when I left Chicago I couldn't even drive. I kept pulling off the road to weep, weeping for the loss of something I would never find again, weeping for yet another loss in my life, one I couldn't get over this time. And yet how selfish and ridiculous! Julie loved me with every ounce of her being, and always had. How was this fair to her? I loved her with all the intensity I could, but I knew it wasn't the same as what she gave to me, and never could be.

I wept all the way home, and then, turning off at my exit, set a steely resolve to box it all up and never look at it again.

And that's what I was doing in the closet when Julie walked in and asked how my day had gone. "Just fine," I replied. "How was work?" she asked. "The usual," I said. "What do you want to do tonight? Do you want to go out for dinner?"

"David. I know you didn't go to work today. You went to Chicago. Your office staff told me you canceled your clinic."

I just looked at her and kept hanging up my suit.

"I think you're in love with Mark," she said, matter-of-factly. "I called him."

And that was the beginning of the end of that chapter of my life. To this day, I wonder what would have happened had she never known I went to Chicago that day. Would she ever have told me about the journal? Or would she just have waited? Would I have survived my decision to box it all up and put it away again, or would I have killed myself as I imagined doing? And what then? What of my sons? What is one to do when all the moves in the game are wrong, when every single choice leads to more pain? What then? What does one do when faced with the reality that any decision you make is going to hurt everyone in some way?

I can't talk about the pain of the ensuing weeks even to this day. It almost killed us both. Julie's slow realization that she had to give me up in order to save me, my realization that I had to help her do it for my sake and for hers. The process was simplified by a good therapist but not made any easier by the knowledge acquired. We spent six months with the therapist and made a plan before we ever talked to the boys and explained how everything was going to be.

So, we all started over, and Julie and I did what we promised each other to the best of our abilities – raising our boys together and protecting them while trying to heal ourselves. At first, we were so sad, just so sad. But life unexpectedly went on, as it always does when tragedy strikes. The world didn't fall apart even though it felt like it. Our own Modern Family *grew up and adjusted. We communicated. We started over. But it wasn't easy, as there are always consequences, and there are always things that a person can't truly get over.*

BEYOND THE HORIZON ———

"Hey Mom – look at this thing I got in the mail. It looks sort of neat. I think I want to go."

"What is it?" Mom asked.

"Well, it looks like a sort of science camp with a bunch of kids my age. It's at someplace called Rose-Hulman Institute of Technology in Terre Haute, Indiana. I don't really know where that is, but it looks like fun."

"I don't know, David. That's awfully far away and it's right in the middle of the summer. I'm not sure your dad will want you to go. He needs your help around here."

"I know, Mom, but look – it's the first three weeks of July. It says right here that I'm 'the kind of student they are looking for.' All we have to do in July is cultivate corn, and Dad can do that without my help. It just takes one guy. And he can do most of the work on the windmill by himself right now too. It's a perfect time for me to be away, if I'm going to be gone. I just have to figure out how to get there. It doesn't cost very much. I really want to go."

Mom looked at the flier.

"Well, why don't you fill it out, and I'll talk to your dad about it. I don't see what harm it would do, though he won't want to spend the money."

Dad never wanted to spend money on us kids, or Mom, and his penny-pinching only got worse as we got older and our needs really started costing something. He was not poor; in fact, most of the surrounding community thought the Costers were rich. But Dad had a spending problem; he spent as much as he wanted to on his farm and all its accouterments. Ask for an ice cream sandwich, though, and "It costs too much" would be the answer. Ask for a new pair of jeans and "You don't need them" would be the answer. So, asking for an instrument for the high school band, a car, a special event, or anything else that cost real money was a waste of time. Unless, of course, it was his idea in the first place. Then it was fine. He came home one day with a Ford Pinto for Angela on her sixteenth birthday. We couldn't believe it. And when he found out they explode with a rear-end collision (thanks, Ralph Nader) he just shrugged. "Don't get rear-ended, Angela."

Dad gave away enormous amounts of cash to shady characters who saw him as an easy target for investment schemes, and he ended up in some real messes as a result, including a trial where one of his "friends" was charged with intention to murder another one of his "friends" and was sent off to prison. He would go to the bank and borrow the money against the farm, sometimes as much as $60,000 for these investment schemes proposed by Des Moines charlatans. Inevitably, he would lose it all and then have to try to find a way to make it up. He made it up by making sure he spent no significant money on his kids. His naivete eventually forced the bank to put all of the farms in irrevocable trusts, with the money to be managed by someone else, a move which created even more problems down the road, but that's another story.

Occasionally, though, especially when the thing desired revolved around education, Mom would step in and somehow save the day. I don't know how she did it, but I got a "yes" this time, and I was thrilled beyond measure. I would be going to the science camp! But first I had to find a way to get there. A visit by Mom to the travel agent got me a cheap airplane ticket, and off I went.

Iowa was so pretty from the air, I mused, leaning with my face pressed against the window of the little Cessna, flying for the first time. The fields below stretched to the hazy horizon like a green patchwork quilt, broken here and there by the glint of the sun on rivers, streams, and ponds; little jewels in the fabric. So, this is where I live. It's beautiful.

I wondered what the people were doing in the towns down there. Sipping their morning coffee, stretching under the covers, going to the park? Little farmhouses dotted the landscape; I knew what the people were doing there – the moms were mopping floors and doing laundry, preparing a mid-morning coffee time snack, making lists of things they needed from the store, reviewing the list of machine parts they had to pick up for their husbands at John Deere, and fretting with the little ones under their feet who couldn't seem to ever get out of the way. So much to do. I could see the toy tractors going across the fields, the dads all cultivating corn today. That's what dads did in July – cultivated and waited for rain, always looking at the sky, noticing the little changes in humidity, the smell of the air, the shift in the breeze, the telltale signs of impending storms, and the little airplanes flying by with nosy people watching them. "It's going to rain today," they would say. And it did. Somehow, they always knew. I knew too. Reading the sky and the land, that's what we farmers did. We learned it not in books, but in our bones, where it seeped in from constant exposure to the elements. We were part of the earth and sky; we could sense the breath and blood of them.

I stretched a little in the cramped space and watched the propeller. "I wonder what would happen if one of those blades flew off and cut me in two." I pondered the scene: the blade coming through so quickly I didn't notice, hearing the roar of the wind through the tear in the plane, looking down to see myself still in the seat, but my lower half lying uselessly on the floor, my gasp of surprise, wondering what to do with my guts trying to squirm out in the seat, and then, finally, the thankful loss of consciousness and slumping over in my seat, my torso falling on the floor too because the seatbelt had nothing left to attach to. I shuddered. It could happen.

How odd it was to be flying through the air, eating pretzels, as if it were normal. Poking around in clouds, my hair not even messed up. It was just so weird to think about. How fast were we going, anyway?

Illinois looked like Iowa, only flatter with even more perfect road grids, and so did Indiana. Miles and miles of crops, all those dads working on them down there.

I picked up my bag at the bottom of the airplane steps. Someone met me and we got in the car and took the short drive to Rose-Hulman. A real college. They studied physics, chemistry, math, engineering, and biology here – "hard" science, they called it. The real stuff. It was a boys' school; there was a girls' college up the road where the Rose-Hulman boys spent as much time as possible, so I was told.

My roommate was a hideous, maladjusted kid with giant hair, pimples, a pear-shaped body, thick glasses, and an annoying penchant for talking about absolutely nothing but physics in his deep, nasal voice. A truer nerd never existed. I had hoped for a handsome, smart, and interesting guy with a sense of humor. Instead, I watched in horror as frizz-head chomped his bedtime snack with his mouth open, rubbery lips smacking, while expounding on his own personal theory of thermodynamics. "I could smother you with your own pillow, you know," I thought to myself, watching him and imagining how easy it would be, his pathetically soft body no match for my own muscle. Something needed to make him shut up.

We were divided into groups on our first day. My group, with Mike and Will, was to do a three-week experiment on corrosion. We had to design the study and perform the experiment and give both written and verbal reports on the next to last day of the session. It was a boring project but we attacked it with gusto, writing out the plan, burying the various metal tubes, daily pouring various liquids down the access pipes and measuring changes in metal impedance through the wires attached, looking for miniscule changes in resistance that might suggest damage to the metal.

We had a lot of free time since our data collection only took us about thirty minutes per day, so we hung out with the other boys, swam in the lake, swung on the rope swings, and stayed up all night playing games and running around the campus. I soon found my own little crowd with whom I became inseparable. We were loud and boisterous and funny, playing pranks and generally being the center of the universe.

At home, I was always a square peg in a round hole, never quite fitting into any group at school at all. At least it felt that way. Here, it was different. Everyone was smart and almost everyone was fun. What few idiosyncrasies I had didn't seem to matter; everyone but two people liked me and thought I was fun and neat, and they wanted to hang out with me. I realized that the world was bigger than I thought.

And then, I developed a terrible crush on Mike Van Beek.

Mike was a big, hunky, handsome redhead from Wisconsin, a football player type, broad-shouldered and lanky, freckle-faced, and he just about did me in. We spent every day together, talking, working, and playing, and I fell farther and farther into him, my heart aching every time I looked at him. There he was in those jeans; there he was in those swim trunks; look at him lying there on the beach at the campus pond. His red hair did a neat little flip onto his forehead. His teeth were whitey-white. He talked about his girlfriend at home. Apparently, she was pretty great.

I'd never had a crush on a boy before. One evening we hiked up to another lake on campus, and Mike, Will, and another buddy of ours decided it would be fun to strip naked and swim across the lake. "But what about our clothes?" I responded in a panic. Thinking about Mike's naked, muscular body slicing the water next to my own for the fifteen minutes it would take to swim across made my stomach lurch. "We'll have to run back around the lake naked to get them! It's a long way, and what if someone catches us? It would be terrible!"

"I'll carry the clothes around," Will piped up. "I'm a bad swimmer. I'm not going to do it."

That left me, Mike, and the other kid. Mike and the other kid started stripping – shirts, shoes, and pants. "Uh, I think I'll go with Will," I said. Seeing Mike almost naked was causing such a sensation in my gut I was about to throw up, and I had such an erection I couldn't bear it. I was getting dizzy. "I don't feel very good, I'm afraid I'll drown," I said weakly. "Here, just give me your clothes." Mike, unembarrassed, took off his underwear and handed me his clothes, plunking the shoes down on top. He was as beautiful as I was afraid he'd be, and completely unashamed, dancing around in his nakedness. I stared, but only for a second. "Let's go, Will. We have to walk a lot farther than they have to swim. We don't want them to get to the other side and be without their clothes."

I hated myself as we ran around the lake. Whatever was my problem, I had to get over it. Mike was my friend, and that was all. Just my best friend.

We all, of course, got into trouble for swimming in the lake, or being an accomplice. A boy who was jealous of the popularity of our little group had told on us.

I took to hanging out with Will a little more after that, instead of Mike all the time. Will was a tiny, unassuming kid, very nice, and plain. I was safer with a boy like that. In looking back now, I always after that episode avoided men I found attractive, whenever possible, just to be safe.

One day, Will and I went to the main building to check our mail. There was an Indiana thunderstorm brewing in the distance; we needed to hurry to keep from getting wet. We ran all the way, taking shortcuts we knew, eventually racing across the small quad in front of the building. "Oh good," Will said, "a letter from my mom." "Me too!" I replied, closing the little door to the mailbox with a slam. It was great to get mail.

Just then we heard the rain come in big sheets, tearing at the windows. "How are we going to get out of here?" Will asked. We opened the door. It was a downpour. "I say we just run for it," I replied. "On the count of three. One, two, three!" I pushed Will out the door in front of me. Just then, a massive bolt of lightning stabbed the fountain in the center of the quad, forty feet away, blinding in intensity. The force of the sonic boom knocked Will backward into me like a rag doll, smashing me against the door, the two of us rolling onto the cement floor in a heap.

I thought Will was dead. He was limp, laying there on top of me. His eyes were closed.

"Will!" I yelled, pushing him onto the floor.

"Will!" No response. I slapped him across the face.

"You better not be dead!" I commanded. He moaned a little. So, I slapped him again. "Wake up!"

His eyes fluttered open, unrecognizing. He stared at me for a few seconds, awareness slowly reemerging. "What happened?" he choked.

"We almost got struck by lightning," I said. "It knocked us back into the building. It's a good thing the door was still open a little or I think we'd both be dead on the step right now. That electricity would have followed the water on the ground right into us. Here, let me help you up."

I pulled him up to a sitting position, where he stayed for a moment, before letting me help him up all the way. I propped him up on the door, waiting for his strength to come back. No one else was in the building. "Are you going to be okay?" I asked. "Yeah, just give me a minute," he said, taking some big breaths. "That really hurt." "I know," I said. "It about killed me, and I had you as a cushion! I can't imagine how you feel. Keep breathing. Move your arms around a little." I looked carefully at his eyes. He seemed to be okay.

"Are you strong enough to run again?"

"I think so."

"Okay, let's go, on the count of three. One, two, three!"

And off we went.

The last day of camp came. Our experiment was a moderate success, our presentation met with humor and catcalls from our crowd of buddies. The professors thought we did just fine. At the end of all the presentations, the dean asked us to do one last thing: "Fill out this form with the name of the person here who you would most like to have in your own school. It's the science camp citizenship award. Every summer we honor one student in this way. We think the students themselves should decide who is the best amongst them."

I looked at Mike. "Did you know we had to do this?" I asked. "Nope," he replied, taking his sheet.

"I'm putting you down," I said. He looked at me in surprise. "I'm not kidding. I think you're the neatest guy here." He still looked surprised. "Well, then I'm putting you down," he said back.

So, we wrote each other's names down, and along with the other sixty students, turned in the sheets. A few minutes later, the dean called for quiet.

"This year's winner for the citizenship award, the young man this group would most like to have in their own school and community, is David Coster. David, would you please come up to receive your award?"

I sat frozen in my chair. I finally fit somewhere; here, with these fun, interesting, and smart young men. I wasn't a misfit. And Dad was wrong; I wasn't worthless either. All I had done was be myself, and they all liked me. I looked around; everyone was beaming at me expectantly, and they started clapping and hollering. I blinked back my surprised tears, pushed my hair out of my eyes, and wound my way through the crowd, everyone slapping me on the back. The dean squeezed my shoulder, handed me a signed certificate, and said "Good job, young man. I hope you come back."

I went back to school that fall with a newfound confidence. I had a goal, and I knew I could do it. I would not be a farmer. I would be a scientist.

I called Mike a couple times that summer after I got back home. He was funny as always, but busy with football practice and his girl. I wonder where he is now.

PLEIADES ——————————

The day in 1970 when my youngest sister Ev was born, Dad came home from the hospital, head in hands, moaning. "Five girls! Five girls in a row! I can't believe it!" He wasn't counting the two oldest. He seemed to have forgotten that he had seven daughters, not five. Seven daughters! Only two sons! Who would take over his farms in his old age?

Dad came from a traditional background. He believed that sons should follow in the footsteps of their fathers, and daughters should find a good husband and be content to be homemakers. These opinions were imposed in various ways, from outright declarations to innuendo. It was, he believed, imperative that his daughters be beautiful, smart, and talented, and thankfully they were. They were all expected to grow up, snag good husbands, and have lots of kids. Neal and I were to grow up and become farmers and have a lot of sons of our own, and that was all there was to it. But Dad had BIG plans for his farms, and he really needed more sons to do the work; he didn't have enough with just Neal and me, thus his despair.

Don't get me wrong; he loved his daughters very much. He thought they were the top of the heap, the cream of the crop, and they were. He did not, however, have any idea he was harming them by demanding they each grow up to be only a certain sort of woman. They were praised for being at the top of their class, but discouraged from further education or careers. He was obsessed with the importance of beauty as a marker of good breeding and as a key to obtaining a great husband. There was no way the girls could expect to grow effortlessly into a modern world with the cognitive dissonance of traditional expectations learned from their parents versus incredible personal abilities and talents that urged them to do something else. The church reinforced Dad's opinion. There was no way they could develop any worldview beyond it. And of course there was always the problem that they were not boys, a fact which was brought up repeatedly. The way Dad treated Mom all those years implied that she was not valued for her intellect, thoughts, or ideas. The impact of watching this less than desirable relationship dynamic seriously affected the way my sisters viewed themselves and their role in the world. It affected their self-esteem and inhibited their abilities to think in a new way, smart as they were. They were all in trouble the instant they were born and didn't even know it.

Dad, with his master plan for his daughters, was particularly worried about Sandy. Where would she find a husband? At her birth, three years previously, the doctor – in a rush to get to a social engagement – performed a high forceps delivery to hurry the process along, a rather silly maneuver considering she was Mom's tenth delivery. In the process, he managed to clamp a little too hard on her skull, pushing a piece of bone into her brain. As a result, she suffered from what they called cerebral palsy, though in reality it was a simple doctor-imposed brain injury. It was as if she'd had a stroke on her right side. That arm was relatively useless, and she walked with a limp due to a contracted Achilles tendon and poorly developed leg muscles. Thankfully, her intelligence and speech were unaffected. We kids were very protective of her, but Dad was very hard on her. He didn't understand why she couldn't get over the injury, and as she grew older he took to making sarcastic fun of her as a way of "encouraging" her to compensate for her injury. When that didn't work, the minister at the church convinced Mom and Dad that God would heal her if they just prayed hard enough, so every Sunday she was dutifully carried up to the altar and anointed with oil, the minister laying hands on her and begging God to repair her broken body. So, she grew up with verbal abuse and taunting from her father at home plus false expectations and chronic religious abuse at church. No one thought to take her to a specialist who could help her. The kids at school mocked her, limping along beside her, holding their arms in a stroke posture and taunting her. If any of us heard about it we would nearly throttle the perpetrators, it made us so mad.

Dad believed only in God and chiropractors, but what Sandy needed of course was a good orthopedic surgeon. She suffered the consequences of Dad's foolishness, Mom's unfounded faith that God would spontaneously heal her, and the inane church teaching that if we just had *more* faith, God would heal her. She was in her twenties before she got what she really needed, and that was only because I kept shaming Mom and Dad for relying on a God that clearly had better things to do than look after my sister. Dr. Grundberg moved some tendons around and *ta-da!* Suddenly her hand worked and she could walk properly. Ridiculously easy. And God had nothing to do with it, just like he had nothing to do with the injury in the first place. Caused by man, fixed by man.

Well, anyway, where was I? A lot happened after Ev was born. Our family was under assault due to the emotional and psychological wars of our parents' past, our church with its angry Christian Evangelicals, the social milieu of the '60s and '70s in which we lived, and the unforeseen circumstances of the future caused by our past and present; but we didn't know it. Neal's death was only the eye of what proved to be a big hurricane that hung on for a long time.

The week of Neal's death I was informed by Dad that I would have to take Neal's place on the farm; any personal goals or aspirations of my own were no longer viable; I was now the oldest son, at twelve, and had duties inherent to the title. He needed me to be a farmer and had compelled me to work in the fields with him beginning at age nine, which is the year I learned to drive the pickup, the small tractor, and the riding lawn mower. It was the wrong thing for me, his plan, but I was too young and too devastated to argue. He had decided.

A few months later, in January of 1973, Jonathan was born; finally, another boy. We were ecstatic; perhaps things were about to change for the better.

And then in April of 1974, a year and a half after Neal died, my cousin and best friend, Tony Felsing, was accidentally killed. He was only twelve. I was digging parsnips at the time, hacking away at the freshly thawed garden soil out back of the house, enjoying the fresh spring smells and early afternoon sunshine. One of my sisters ran up to me and announced that Tony was dead, accidentally shot in the heart by a classmate. I hesitated only a moment before looking down and stabbing the garden fork back into the soil. Stab, turn... stab, turn...stab, turn. Methodically, I continued to flip parsnips, staring at the black dirt for the next fifteen minutes, as if I'd heard nothing. This couldn't possibly be true.

The details? It was such a nice morning; Tony and his chum decided to play hooky from school, taking Uncle Arthur's .22 rifle out to shoot sparrows. Thinking the gun was empty now, and being silly, Tony laughingly told the guy to pretend to shoot him in the heart as he danced around foolishly in the meadow. Neither knew there was still a bullet in the rifle. It passed cleanly through Tony's heart, dropping him to the ground with only a little "Ohhh!" And that was it. The guy ran screaming to his mother, "I killed Tony, I killed Tony!" but at first no one believed him. They thought it was a joke, but just in case, they called Aunt Joyce, who ran to the field and found her little son lying dead in the grass.

So once again, I found myself walking down a church aisle to another casket containing another boy I loved, but this time the casket was open. I didn't want to look, but I had to. I walked right up to the casket, the white satin gleaming behind Tony's face. He had his summer buzz cut, like always. His face was swollen, I noticed. Once again, I turned and went to my seat in the family section. The burial was just as jarring as it had been with Neal, the casket being lowered into a hideous hole in the ground. The idea of him being locked in a box in the ground was just terrible to me. I didn't know there were alternatives.

Tony's classmate never recovered from the shock of what he'd done. His life was ruined too.

Angela was a senior in high school in August of 1973, the first one to finish! She was beautiful, smart, and talented. The valedictorian of her class, she played at least ten instruments fluently, was a gifted artist, was active in the community, and was considered to be superb college material. I couldn't wait to see which university she chose! It was so exciting and frightening, this idea of going far away to meet new people and learn new things. I was so anxious for her to pave the way. The oldest of our clan! She was marvelous! What would she be? An accountant? A pianist? A country music performer in Nashville? A college professor? The president? She could do anything. She really could!

A couple weeks after a May graduation in 1974 and a few days after her eighteenth birthday, however, she got married. She and Lavern settled into a little old house on the south end of our farm. In the absence of any fully capable adult Coster sons, Lavern began farming with Dad. So did Angela, working around the clock running tractors and taking care of her house and husband. Three children were born. Marital difficulties developed. It was all so predictable. She chafed at the traditional restraints of her farmwife life. So many hopes dashed, so many personal expectations not met. Angela was the first to begin the struggle of adulthood with the leftover baggage of her youth, but not the last.

Mary Ann had the voice of an angel; people sobbed as she sang, the notes tearing their little hearts right from their chests. She was beautiful and had the body of a goddess; the sort of look that caused traffic accidents. She snagged herself a handsome, bad-assed, silver-tongued Texan devil named Mark. He was up visiting his grandmother for just the summer, but that didn't matter; she dug her claws into him so far, he wasn't going anywhere. And Dad didn't like it – not one bit; stupid pot-smokin' lyin' Texan. "Get rid of him," Dad said. "And I mean it!"

But the Texan stayed and went to high school so he could be with Mary Ann, and the more Dad hollered about it, the more Mary Ann dug in her heels. Mom thought it might all be okay, as long as the Texan went to church and got saved, so he did. Supposedly. But Dad still didn't buy it, and he and Mary Ann fought and fought. So finally, Mary Ann won by purposefully getting pregnant so she could marry her Texan, which she did in November. She dropped out of school and moved to St. Louis where her hubby joined the Air Force. Marital difficulties ensued, of course, but she met the goal Dad set for her; she snagged a man. And as long as he was saved, Mom was fine with it.

And then, at fourteen and a half, I was the oldest son and the oldest child still at home; I felt like an old man already.

Mary Ann had her baby on my fifteenth birthday that next summer; Mom was forty and about to be pregnant again, but she didn't yet know it.

"I wonder why Mom isn't home," Nancy mused as we threw our books on the dining room table. "She said she'd be here."

I paused and listened for a moment. The only sound was the clock ticking and the gears of the school bus grinding off in the distance.

I didn't know why Mom wasn't home. She'd been having a really hard time lately. For the previous year, she'd been home very little, choosing instead to spend her time in church or running around with her friends, Betty and Alice. Without Angela and Mary Ann around, Nancy and I, now thirteen and fifteen, had become the de facto parents for Kathy, Julie, Sandy, Ev, and Jonathan, and we weren't doing a very good job. We accused Mom of abandoning us, which only made her angry and depressed and caused her to stay away even more. Dad hollered at her for being gone all the time. The more he hollered, the more she ran around with her friends, coming home late at night and sometimes not at all, preferring instead to stay overnight at Betty's or going to Des Moines to stay at a nice hotel to get away from her life.

The church was her other refuge. Without fail there was always someone there "in need" of her help, someone suffering more than Mom, more than us; it was they who got her attention. We got into big fights about it, accusing Mom of being so "heavenly minded she was of no earthly good," but that only made her cry and yell at us. God needed her worse than we did; the church needed her worse than we did. "I have to go to church," was the default response to every request for attention. "You kids can stay home. There are bottles in the fridge for Jonathan."

We begged her to stay home. "Mom, you're gone all the time! We need you here!"

"I'll be back in a few hours. Stop your bawling."

And out the door she went, leaving Ev and Jonathan wailing away, Sunday morning, Sunday night, Wednesday night, Thursday night. There was always something important going on at The Church. By now, I hated that fucking church for taking our mother, the one person whom we once had been able to count on.

Dad, out working until nine or ten p.m., was just plain mean and cranky whenever he came in, and completely unavailable as a parent. He raised nary a finger to help us.

Ev had turned into a mouthy, independent, defiant, self-reliant five-year-old whom we couldn't control. We worried constantly about Sandy's arm and leg; she required help with a lot of things. Julie and Kathy just did what they wanted and seemed relatively unfazed by the situation. We all lived on Fortified Oat Flakes, ice cream, and eggs fried in an inch of

Crisco, as we had begun doing when Mom had her cooking meltdown.

One night, still fourteen, I found myself crying, out of fear and frustration, when it was so late and I was so tired I couldn't see straight, and I couldn't get little Jonathan to go to sleep in his crib. Dad was asleep and snoring like a freight train and couldn't be roused. He wouldn't have helped anyway. My homework wasn't done. I was exhausted. Yet I worried what it must have felt like to be Mom, dealing with crying babies almost every night for the previous twenty years; I had great sympathy for her. I never told her how scared I was to be taking care of such little ones alone at that age.

Occasionally, Mom took us with her to Betty's house where we played with Betty's kids and her pet skunk, Petunia. One night we had a wreck on the way, crashing into a car that turned in front of our van, but Mom was so intent on getting away from her life that she just looked at the damage, exchanged phone numbers with the other driver, and went on as if nothing happened. All we wanted was to go home at that point, but she just didn't care. She had friends to meet.

Mom spent so much time with Betty and Alice that Dad finally accused her of being a lesbian. I found out years later in an off-the-record intimate conversation with my mother that Betty and Alice actually *were* lesbians, and indeed took Mom to a lesbian bar in Des Moines, shortly after she learned that she was pregnant yet again, to cheer her up. Mom was in a real funk that night, and uncharacteristically smoked a cigarette while wondering what she was doing with her life; another child in her womb at that very moment, another twenty years of child-rearing ahead of her. At age forty, she'd hit rock bottom.

Apparently, that night at the bar, a turning point was reached. A friendly woman made an overture in Mom's direction, which really put her off. It was only then, after really studying the room, that she realized Dad was right. Mom had thought it was weird there were no men there, but due to her naivete, she had no idea she was in a lesbian bar, even as Alice and Betty danced away on the dance floor with all the other women. It was the night that she finally looked intensely at her predicament and decided to abandon Alice and Betty and give up on her effort to escape her life. The web at home was too strong, and she couldn't get out of it, this trap she'd unintentionally made. She just had to suck it up and go back home and live out the life she had concocted for herself. Put up the walls, hide the emotions and thoughts, and just do her job. She put out her cigarette and demanded to be taken home so she could retreat completely into her despair. I will never have a complete understanding of how she felt. Three dead sons, a verbally abusive husband who only cared about food and sex and tractors and having more sons, so many kids to raise with virtually no assistance she couldn't actually successfully do it, her original hopes for a career and interesting life dashed, her every move sarcastically criticized by her all-observant husband, her second daughter already in a bad marriage at seventeen, with a little baby, and herself pregnant for the thirteenth time. She'd given her life to God and given her children up for God – the supreme sacrifice to a God who's never satisfied. But, He predictably failed to notice and gave her nothing in return.

Now, a few weeks after the bar episode, not knowing the

half of it, I was standing in the kitchen wondering where she'd gone this time. Jonathan was napping in his bed so she couldn't have been gone long, but she normally wouldn't go out like that and leave a two-and-a-half-year-old at home unattended. Maybe Dad was supposed to be watching him, I thought. I was worried though. Mom had been unusually quiet just recently. I often came home from school to find her eyes swollen from crying, her posture slumped. She wouldn't look at me and barely responded when I tried to talk to her. It was obvious she hated Dad; their interactions had taken on a vicious tone. The house was a mess and she didn't care. She relied on us to do as much as possible. She just wanted to sleep, and she didn't want to have this baby.

"She must have gone to town for something from the store," I shrugged. "Let's put our stuff away and get something to eat," I said to Nancy.

I sauntered into my room, pulling my shirt off over my head as I went through the door, casually tossing it on the back of the desk chair. "Funny," I thought. "I didn't leave all that stuff on my dresser; where did it come from?" Frowning, I took a step closer. There was a note on top.

David,

I'm leaving you these things. I don't know if I'll ever be back. Please take care of the little ones.

I love you,

Mom

About then, I heard a shriek from Nancy's room. I knew she'd found something too. I quickly walked into Kathy's room, only to find another shrine on her dresser with all sorts of jewelry, clothes, and personal items left as mementos. There was a note for her too. There were notes for everyone, with piles of the belongings that mattered to her the most.

Dad got a note too; a big one, without any gifts.

For the next few days, Dad stayed in the house while the rest of us, except Jonathan, went to school, waiting for Mom to return. We thought she would come back, but she did not reappear soon as Dad promised she would. No letters, no phone calls. Dad's requests for information from Mom's sisters and Grandma Felsing went unanswered. They said they didn't know where she was either. He drove around looking for her when we were home from school each day, blaming us for her disappearance. "When she gets back, you kids better behave for a change and help around here!" he hollered at us.

"Maybe YOU should," I muttered under my breath.

Days went by. We went to school. We couldn't imagine that Mom could really go away and leave us, particularly the younger ones – Sandy, Ev, and Jonathan. Didn't she miss them? Didn't she know they couldn't live without their mother?

By Thursday, I began to resign myself to her absence. "Good for her," I thought. "This will teach Dad a lesson for being so mean to her all these years. Serves him right." But I hoped she'd come and get the youngest three. They needed her, and I couldn't properly raise them. "Please, please," I thought, "at least come back for them." The rest of us, at least, were all ten or older, and I figured we could get by until we grew up. I resolved to stay as long as it took to get everyone safely grown up, but my anger with Dad by this time knew no bounds. He was making me become the dad, and Nancy the mom, and it just wasn't right.

And then on Friday, I got off the bus as usual. It had been an exceptionally long week at school. "Hey," Nancy said, as we began trudging to the house with Kathy, Julie, Sandy and

Ev. "Isn't that Mom's car?"

I squinted. Yep, it was.

We ran screaming to the house, the girls bawling. "Mom, Mom!" We beat down the door, only to be met by Dad, with Mom nowhere in sight. "Where's Mom?" we asked breathlessly, looking wildly about. "She's asleep, and you guys had better be quiet!" Dad seethed. "It took me all day to convince her to stay, and I'm still not sure she will! If EVERYBODY doesn't make some changes around here, she'll be gone in a second!" He then laid down the law on the conditions Mom had placed upon us for her continued sojourn at the Coster farmstead, emphasizing our blame for the situation. He said nothing of his own complicity in the situation.

The house was pretty quiet for a long time after that, and my once-upon-a-time vivacious and happy Mom was now permanently serious. For once, Dad actually treated Mom like she mattered, helping her around the house and being careful with his choice of words, but she remained sullen. She never believed it would last, and the last bit of love she may have had for him had evaporated. As for us, we kept our rooms cleaned and helped her and did what she said and reminded her every day how happy we were she was there. We were too young and emotionally blind to understand Mom's suffering or comprehend that she had been — and would continue — slowly wilting away from depression. But she knew she had to pull herself together and get ready for the next baby, and that's what she resolved to do.

In April of 1976, she finally had her last baby. A C-section this time, wouldn't you know. Joey weighed in at ten pounds and was a whopping twenty-four inches long, a veritable monster. He was too big to come out, and Mom and her uterus were just too tired to try. And then she got a staph infection and had to stay in the hospital for almost three weeks, unable to hold her baby, weeping her head off as little Joey went home with us kids instead of with her, the last straw. "We'll take good care of him, Mom. Don't worry!" we promised, crying ourselves because we couldn't stand to see Mom cry in the doorway of her hospital room, and we didn't know when or if she would ever come home.

Mary Ann came home from St. Louis for a while to help since Mom couldn't leave the hospital. It was spring planting time and Dad couldn't stay in the house to help. Mary Ann knew what to do with Joey, and we were glad for her presence, especially when Joey's umbilical cord stump fell off too soon and we could look inside him and see his intestines working. The doctor said it was nothing to worry about, just put a band-aid on it until it closes up in a couple of days; and so we did.

Then Julie got appendicitis, and Sandy got thrown off the horse, breaking her good arm, so Mom got to have at least some of her family in the hospital with her to keep her company through the doorway, and all we could do at that point was laugh at how ridiculous everything had become. It was the hysterical crazed laughter of near-psychosis, mixed with tears.

Mom finally came home to great fanfare, picking up her little Joey and hugging him almost to death. She cried as Jonathan climbed onto her lap too, and everyone else surrounded and hugged her. We loved our mother more than anything.

Mom eventually began to recover a little emotionally, but she never went back to being the happy-go-lucky mom of my early years, as she'd given up on too many things she needed, but acceptance of one's circumstances can go a long way toward a sort of peace. She relied more and more heavily on her faith, but she refocused it, turning in to her own natural goodness and desire to do something productive for others as part of her self-healing. We never really got what we needed from her, though, as she had always had a tendency to leave us to rely on our own abilities once we could walk – she was attached only to the babies. But even the baby attachment was no match for God. He got nearly all of her love and attention for the rest of her life. I hope He appreciated it. His greediness did a lot of damage.

That summer after Joey's birth – 1976 – when I was sixteen, Dad decided to hire Herald Kelderman to do an addition on our house. Herald would be the contractor; Dad, my friend Ed (Neal's best friend from childhood with whom we had kept in contact), and I would be the laborers. It was a dumb project considering that we'd gotten along just fine with the house as it was, and now the kids were all growing up and leaving, but Dad wanted it done anyway.

It became clear shortly into the project that we needed some extra help, so Herald, being the Christian man he was, hired a poor paroled convict who needed some work and a new start in life. He explained the desperate circumstances of the idiot's life to Mom, who, bless her heart, decided that God wanted her to give the poor soul a place to stay.

In my room, of course.

So, Duane Allgood came to live with me. He helped build our house addition while Mom helped construct a soul for him.

Duane smoked like a chimney. He was a little, smelly, wiry blond dude with sunken cheeks and big tattooed biceps. He listened patiently as Mom worked on his inner child, slowly working the magic of her ministry on him, waiting patiently for Jesus to awaken his spirit, each day doing more, laying the seeds that would eventually set root in his soul and save him, just like the Church taught her to do.

Meanwhile, I was dying of emphysema in my own bedroom. I had the top bunk, so Duane's cigarette smoke all ended up enveloping my head each night. I choked and gagged and politely suggested he smoke outside before he went to bed, but he'd have none of it. I finally told Mom that I didn't care what Jesus said about it, Duane was just going to have to go to hell. I wanted that bitch out of my room!

"Now, David. You know what the Bible says about our responsibilities to take care of those in need..."

"Well, yeah, Mom, but that doesn't mean you have to kill me in the process! What the hell are you doing? That guy's *smoking* me to death! And he stinks to high heaven! The son-of-a-bitch hasn't had a bath in a year! Even Jesus would throw him out, Mom, for Christ's sake!"

"Young man, you stop talking like that!" she replied.

"Well, goddammit, Mom, I'm not kidding! It's either him or me! Make your choice!"

So, she picked Duane. That's what God wanted.

But wait! A mere two days later, Herald overheard Duane talking on the phone to a friend about how much he wanted to screw my sisters. He'd been watching them for weeks and he thought he'd get his chance sooner or later.

Herald told Dad. Dad told Mom.

And Duane was gone so fast he didn't know what hit him, the son-of-a-bitch.

"I told you!" I hollered at Mom. "That bastard's name should have been Duane All BAD, not Duane All GOOD! I can't believe you let him lay there and wreck my lungs all this time! Good grief, even God can't fix an idiot like that! Don't you EVER bring another one of those creeps into my room! Geez, the girls are lucky they weren't all raped and murdered!"

At eighty-eight she still hasn't learned her lesson. She still thinks everyone can be salvaged.

As for me, I learned that some people simply aren't worth saving, and some just can't be saved.

Meanwhile, Ed – Neal's best friend from school – fell in love with Nancy while he was helping us build the addition on our house. By the next summer, they'd been dating for a year already. Nancy was just fifteen; Ed was now eighteen and freshly graduated from high school, their relationship moving along at a rapid pace.

One morning in late August, 1977, Nancy walked into the bathroom while I was brushing my teeth, getting ready for school. She sat down around the corner by the vanity.

"I'm getting married in two weeks," she announced calmly.

I choked on my toothbrush, spewing all over the sink. The room momentarily went black.

"You what?" I shrieked, throwing the toothbrush. "Are you out of your mind? What the hell are you talking about? When did you decide that? Do Mom and Dad know? You're only fifteen, you can't go off and get married! What about college? What about your life? Are you insane?"

I sat down with a thud on the side of the tub.

"I'll be sixteen in two weeks..."

"So WHAT!" I interrupted.

"And I already talked to Mom and Dad about it, and they said it would be okay. Dad's aunt got married when she was only fifteen, and she got along just fine."

"SO WHAT!" I explained again.

"If we don't get married, we're going to have sex. We can't help it. And I won't have sex without being married, it's a terrible sin. So, I don't have any choice. I have to get married now."

"NO, YOU DON'T! GO ON THE PILL! Who cares if you have sex? You're too young to decide this! How do you know he's the right guy, Nancy? What about school? What about... EVERYTHING?"

"David, I'm getting married, and you can either be helpful, or be an ass. The wedding is on September ninth, three days after my sixteenth birthday. Ed wants you to stand up with him."

And so, I did. What else could I do?

So, Nancy left, sort of. She missed Mom and the rest of us, so spent a lot of time at the house. Eventually, she and Ed just moved in, because that's what Nancy wanted. She was still a girl and needed her mother, not that being back at home meant she really had one.

OPERATING A SACK ——————

John Coster was nothing if not self-reliant. He could place field tile, repair engines, reconfigure the wiring in the house, replace the plumbing, repair any piece of equipment, weld, run a cutting torch, do carpentry, run all sorts of gadgets, tinker on things, milk a cow, or butcher a hog. He always fixed everything himself if possible. If he couldn't buy what he needed or it was too expensive, he'd cobble something together or make something up that worked anyway. Well, most of the time. The windmill was an exception. And I guess he had a tendency to leave things only partially done, like the patio stairs that were still unfinished twenty-five years after he started them, but never mind. He fully expected me to learn all his tricks and grow up to be a real man one day, a man that could do everything and fix anything. In a word – a farmer.

My brain, however, was resistant to learning mechanics. When learning to drive the stick-shift pickup at nine, in a six-hundred-acre field, mind you, one square mile, I hit the only post in the field and knocked the mirror off. I nearly killed myself one day when I couldn't push the clutch all the way in on the riding lawn mower. It drove me under the John Deere 4400 tractor, nearly taking my head off before my desperate little toes finally got that last quarter-inch of leverage to stop the machine. There I sat, stuck, with my throat against the tractor engine housing, screaming for help.

I couldn't fix an engine to save my life. If the tractor failed while I was cultivating corn, I had no idea what to do about it. I would walk dejectedly to the house and have to admit that I had no idea how to fix the problem. I nearly electrocuted myself, I don't know how many times, while working on wiring or hanging lights, and Dad got so frustrated watching me fumble with wrenches to tighten bolts or take things apart that he'd just say, "Good grief, can't you do anything?"

Thankfully, I wasn't alone. From Dad's perspective, Angela couldn't do anything either. Neither could Mary Ann, Nancy, Kathy, Julie, Sandy, or even Ev. Neal had been the only one who could do anything, and he was gone. So, when Angela tried to pick corn at twenty miles per hour, burning up the clutch and nearly catching the combine on fire, I was glad. It took the criticism off me. And the time she knocked the spout completely off the combine because she didn't see the twenty-foot-tall wagon looming beside her until she heard the spout rip off the machine – I was glad about that too. But I made too many mistakes myself to ever be free of criticism, and my sisters didn't make enough mistakes to keep the heat off me for long. If I knocked over even one stalk of corn while cultivating in a three-hundred-acre patch, somehow Dad would notice it from a half-mile away, walk over to it, and point it out. "You cost me two ears of corn, David. Be more careful, would you?"

My straight A's at school created a tiny refuge of safety, but Dad couldn't figure out how someone so smart could be so dumb when it came to doing farm things. "But I got an A on my college prep paper, Dad," only went so far when I accidentally drove the tractor into the back of the combine and dented up the chaff throwers. "What in the world do you think you're doing, you idiot!"

Dad's sarcasm was generally just sarcasm. But sometimes, he was absolutely vicious about it and outright mean as hell, a real problem for me as I strove to be what he wanted, always failing. There was nearly always a wall of tension between us, a tension so thick that sometimes, in order for us to live in the same space, something had to break it. And laughter was the only antidote powerful enough to do it. Sometimes Dad's sarcasm was just so wickedly sharp or over-the-top that it transcended itself and accidentally became funny.

One day, we were doing the very simple task of filling the planter boxes full of corn seed. It was early May, the usual corn-planting time. My job was to pull the seed bags to the end of the field on a rack so when Dad rolled up with the massive sixteen-row planter, we could quickly fill all the boxes, replace insecticide, inspect the chains and gears, and do a quick general inspection. It was just like a pit stop. Fast, furious, and accurate. And Dad wanted it perfect!

I've always had trouble with knots. Dad wasted enormous effort over the years trying to teach me granny knots, slip knots, square knots, and hangman's nooses, all to no avail. So, every spring, I'd sweat bullets, knowing that all those seed bags were sewn shut with a certain sort of stitch that required finesse to undo. "Let's see, is it that string I pull, or that other one?" I could never get it right. I don't care how many times I saw it, how many times I accidentally got it right, or how many times I pulled the wrong string and created a knot rather than getting the desired result of a quick unzipping of the entire thread and the miraculous opening of the bag, I could never actually remember the steps. This should not have been a difficult task, but then again, I was the last kid to learn to tie my shoes in kindergarten. As Dad was exasperated beyond measure over my knotting skills, I always started opening seed bags on the other end of the planter, where he couldn't watch me fumble with the strings, a coward's approach that sometimes saved me and kept the peace.

On this particular day, though, as I was lurking at the far end of the planter, hiding my incompetence, Dad managed to open and empty, oh, I don't know, maybe ten eighty-pound bags, while I stood there fighting with the strings on *one* bag, trying to hide my stupidity by nonchalantly placing the bag by the wheel where it couldn't be seen, and placing my back to Dad so he couldn't see me struggle.

Well, he saw the whole thing of course. He was watching me out the corner of his left eye the entire time. He waited, and waited, knowing the longer he waited, the more effective his withering denunciation would be.

And then, there it was: a slight pause in activity from Dad's direction, and then the bracing cringe in my head created by the sudden vacuum of sound from his end of the planter, knowing I was about to get it.

"Good grief, David! *Can't you even operate a SACK????!!!*"

I stood quietly, for a second, then laughed until I cried. With one well-strung six-word insult, Dad had managed to encapsulate a lifetime of aggravation with my lack of necessary farming skills. It was brilliant. He was the master.

Soon enough, my laughter got a smile out of him, and then a giggle, and then he was laughing as hard as I was, both of us then bent over in guffaws with tears running down our faces.

What, after all, was a sack operator? How *do* you operate

a sack? Can you operate your way out of a sack? Into a sack? Do you need a degree to operate sacks? How much do sack operators pull down per year?

From then on, "can't you even operate a sack" was our code phrase for ineptitude. It always elicited a laugh, and it was just as fun to use it on him, rare though the chance might be.

YOUNG DRIVERS ────────────

I can think of few things worse than being the parent of ten children and having to teach them all to drive. We had lots of accidents as we navigated behind the wheels of cars and farm machines. Let's see, Mary Ann hung the van up on the rear end of a car right outside the police station in Oskaloosa; Julie bent the Monte Carlo into a "U" when she used it to span a ditch; I put a big dent in the Monte Carlo when I backed into it with Dad's vehicle, and I hit a calf at 90 mph in Dad's car. And never mind the flattened cats, dogs, raccoons, and geese. And the speeding tickets. And always, there was Neal's foolish foray into the path of an oncoming car on the motorcycle. But Jonathan ultimately won the prize for being, perhaps, the world's youngest and most dramatic incompetent driver.

It was a hot day in late June. We were walking beans at the Fremont farm. The rows were a good half-mile long, a lot of work, so we decided to cool off by wading in the creek for a bit before heading back, whacking out volunteer corn and other weeds with our hoes and corn hooks. Herbicides could only do so much. Good old-fashioned kid-power was used for the rest.

We left Jonathan behind in the pickup on the dirt lane in the middle of the field. He was tired of walking beans, being only four, and needed to rest. He was told to nap quietly in the pickup until we returned in a half hour or forty-five minutes, a time that had been extended by at least fifteen minutes while we cooled off in the creek before starting our half-mile walk back to the truck.

We were almost back, just cresting the hill, when all of a sudden, I swore I heard the pickup engine start. "Everyone be quiet!" I ordered. We all stopped and listened. Sure enough, there it was: the sound of an engine revving, and then the distinct sound of the pickup moving away over the hilltop. We all looked at each other, incredulous. Could Jonathan have taken off in the truck? We took off running through the field, cresting the hill just in time to see the pickup driving away toward the farmhouse, weaving in and out of the corn and beans, with the engine revving, and pausing, revving, and pausing. I was in cross-country and basketball the previous year and was in really good shape, but even my long strides sprinting through the field couldn't catch up with him at the clip he was going. "Jonathan! Jonathan!" I hollered, but to no avail. He couldn't hear me.

The girls gradually dropped behind. Dad dropped behind. Eventually even Lavern, Angela's husband, dropped behind. The truck was a quarter-mile beyond me, heading directly for a huge railroad cut placed there a century ago for the trains, a ditch with a precipitous fifteen-foot drop. I was just sick as I watched Jonathan weave his way steadily toward the cut, my legs burning with effort – faster, faster – but it wasn't enough. The pickup disappeared.

I didn't think it possible, but in spite of having already run a half-mile at top speed through loose dirt, I pushed even harder and ran even faster, my lungs heaving with the effort, scared to death that Jonathan was dead in the pickup, rolled over at the bottom of the railroad cut. Or smashed and thrown from the truck, crushed, with broken limbs and blood everywhere. I was alone with my dreadful thoughts. I'd left everyone back in the dust; I was the only one who might help.

I flew to the edge of the cut, expecting the worst, out of breath, eyes wide, but...no truck! What in the world???

A quick glance to the left and there it was, smashed into the side of a big silage wagon, the wagon shoved a good twenty feet by the impact, steam rising from the truck engine. I was at the truck in a heartbeat, peering inside, expecting to find Jonathan's crumpled little body, but there was no one there.

"Where *is* he?" I said to no one. Dead under the wagon? No, not there; dead under the truck? No, not there; dead in the grass? No, not there either. I couldn't see him on the dirt lane to the house either. I'd arrived at the scene within two minutes of the truck disappearing from sight. To where could he have vanished so quickly?

But then, on the ground in the thick dust, I saw what I needed to see: Jonathan's little footprints, toes widely splayed in a dead run, heading up the lane and straight for the house. "That little devil," I thought. "He can't be hurt much if he can run like that!" I had a clear view of the farm lane and I couldn't even see him, so he was already at least an eighth of a mile ahead of me. Geez.

I slowed down and jogged the remaining quarter-mile to Angela's house, seeing nothing but Jonathan's tracks in the dust the entire way. I had no idea such a little kid could run so fast. I stepped onto the porch, pulled open the screen door, and saw Angela working in the kitchen.

"Is Jonathan here?" I asked.

"Yeah, he's in watching TV. He came rushing in here a few

minutes ago and I thought something was wrong, but he said he just got tired of working in the field and decided to come up and watch TV. Is everything okay?"

Without an explanation, I turned on my heel and walked into the living room, where I finally found him, sitting on the couch, staring silently at the TV, about to burst into tears. Poor little kid, scared out of his wits. I knelt in front of him and asked if he was okay, if he was hurt anyplace.

He just looked at me, unable to speak, hoping I didn't know that he'd just crashed the pickup and silage wagon.

Just then, Lavern walked in. "Where's Jonathan?" he asked Angela.

"In the living room. What's going on? Why is everyone looking for Jonathan?"

Lavern was hopping mad at the damage done to the truck and farm equipment and came marching into the living room, hollering at little Jonathan while Angela stood in the background.

"Lay off, Lavern, leave him alone," I snorted. "He's only four! He's scared to death and could've been killed. I think that's pretty much enough for one day, don't you? He knows damn well he shouldn't have done that, and it's over now. So, stop it. He must have thought we all abandoned him, so he did what he knew to do and headed home. It's amazing he's smart enough to drive, just from watching Dad. Not that he *should* be driving, of course." Anyone could see the poor kid needed a big hug and a bowl of soup, not a whipping.

Lavern left, stomping mad. I picked Jonathan up, hugged him and told Angela what happened, so she hugged him too and made him some chicken soup, got him an ice cream sandwich, and spent the rest of the afternoon helping him get over his trauma. Everyone else popped in one by one as they managed to get there, all concerned about this little boy and his accident.

It turned out he *had* thought he'd been abandoned, like me, that day so long ago back in the park, so he just started the truck, put it in gear, slid down the seat to push the accelerator, stood up to see where he was and to adjust the steering, slid down again and pushed the accelerator, and on and on like that until he crashed. He'd watched Dad drive his entire life, he informed me, so he figured it couldn't be *that* hard. Besides, he knew the way to the house.

And that was the day Dad found his new farmer.

"Hey Sam, what are you doing?" I said into my cellphone. I always liked checking in with Sam every morning before school. He was always so funny.

"Well, I'm sitting on the side of the road looking at the pickup upside down in the ditch," he responded.

I frowned for a second, trying to decide if I was being punked or not. "You're such a liar," I finally said, snorting out a laugh. He was always playing tricks on me.

"No, Dad, I'm not kidding. I just rolled the truck. I'm sitting here staring at it."

"Are you alright? Where are you?"

"I'm fine. I just crawled out and sat down when the phone rang. I'm on the gravel road north of Mom's. I crushed the cab."

"I don't care about the damned truck. Are you sure you're okay?"

"Yeah. I was hanging upside down by my seatbelt. I didn't get hurt. I got caught in the gravel on the shoulder and it sucked me into the ditch."

"That ditch is deep right there, Sam."

"Tell me about it!"

"Is your mom still at the house?"

"Yeah."

"Stay right there. I'm calling her to come and get you. She'll be there in two minutes."

FATHERS AND SONS ————————

In the spring of 1978, I once again concluded I really had to go to college. Farming was just not working out for me, as I'd predicted after my foray to Rose-Hulman three years previously. I tried to tell Dad I had to go, but couldn't. He was counting on me to stay on the farm, to "walk in his footsteps," as he put it. He'd planned my life for me, and I didn't know how to tell him it was the wrong plan. I didn't want to hurt him, and I didn't want to disappoint him. He was still in such grief over Neal. My relationship with him seemed complicated. I tried and tried to connect with him but could never get through his veneer to find out who he really was. I wanted him to understand me, and I wanted to understand him. Somehow, I never seemed to get there. I still felt obligated to be Neal. I still felt like the second son.

My fear of the consequences of challenging Dad and leaving the farm had paralyzed me. I had barely talked to the counselor at school, hadn't taken my ACT exam, and really had no idea what to do. No one in my family had ever gone to college.

I was, however, able to talk to Mom about it even if I couldn't talk to Dad. I finally went to the counselor for help in getting registered for the ACT. The date for the exam was right after graduation. Mom kept it a secret from Dad. I don't remember how I managed to get the time off from the farm-work to actually disappear for a day, but Mom must have been party to some story that would relieve me of my farm duties that day. So, not telling Dad, I drove to Indian Hills Community College in Ottumwa, where I took the test one Saturday morning; cold, no preparation.

Six weeks later, I opened an envelope in the mail and looked at my score: 32. It was a great score, but I didn't realize it. With my GPA and that score, I could have gone to any college in the country, and probably on scholarship, but I'd done none of the things one normally does to secure scholarships or other awards; I hadn't even applied to a college. And it was already mid-July.

So, I just decided I would try to go to Evangel College, where all my church friends went. What difference did it make? I just knew I had to open a door somewhere, anywhere, that would get me off that farm. Evangel was a small Christian liberal arts college in Springfield, Missouri. I applied late in July and got a letter of acceptance within a week. I visited the campus one weekend, and Dad allowed it because it was billed as a "youth event" for the church kids – he still didn't know I had been accepted there. We went by bus. The place seemed okay, though the buildings were ramshackle. The campus had once been an army barracks, and many of the classrooms were still in those old army barracks. The Evangelicals who had opened the college were taking their sweet time to bring it up to the expected standards; they had just a few dorms, a gym, and a cafeteria which had been recently built. As I had never been to a campus except once, I didn't have much in mind to compare it to, and the people I met seemed nice enough, though I'd been seriously startled when Gary Clute, a nearly seven-foot tall basketball player already in the dorm because he had to come to campus early for sports, had walked into the dorm room where I sat watching TV with some other early birds, and stepping behind the couch, whipped out his ten-inch cock and calmly laid it across the shoulder of an unsuspecting boy sitting there, scaring him half to death. So that was where I went to college that fall.

That was it. No research, no interviews, no looking at other schools.

Mom secretly paid the tuition of $2,500 for the fall semester.

When I told Dad I was going away to school late that summer after returning from the campus visit three weeks before classes were to start, he was furious and hurt. He didn't want me to leave, and he was wrapped tight until I left. Things went from bad to worse in our relationship. He taunted me and made fun of me, trying his best to shame me into staying home, shame me into being the son he needed, the one he lost. I bore his pained abuse but didn't cave in. For the most part, I just listened quietly, making my mind up, my resolve growing, thinking that it was grief and fear of losing another son that made him treat me so much more badly now, all the while knowing it had always been this way. I couldn't bear to hurt him more by talking about it and I just wanted to avoid a confrontation.

I was so glad to pack up the old '72 Monte Carlo with the few things I had and drive away that fall, but I was wracked with guilt for leaving him behind. It was like the death of another son to him, and I knew it. He had always seemed a desperate man to me. Desperate, at least, about his sons.

So, in spite of my newfound freedom, I was tearful and afraid. During the first couple of months at school, I was so homesick I was literally physically ill. I almost packed up and went back home; but in the end, I decided to stay and see what happened. Everytime I thought of jumping in the car and going back, a nagging feeling that it would be the end of my life kept popping up.

I had no money; Dad never paid me for the work I did on the farm and wouldn't let me get a job in town. I skipped meals and didn't go out in order to keep Mom from having to send money and risk Dad's wrath at home for wasting it on my college education.

I took the CLEP exam and tested out of an entire year of school and started as a sophomore, saving Dad and Mom an entire year's tuition costs. In the end, I was so good at taking extra classes and making straight A's that I finished all the courses for a Biology major, a Chemistry minor, and a concentration in Theology in only three years and at a cost of a measly fifteen-thousand dollars total, a pretty remarkable feat that required constant studying; so I did not get a part-time job.

Evangel was a good school academically; small class size and brilliant, accessible professors led to a great education in my areas of interest. The downside was that the core curriculum of Theology was required and I didn't want to do it, and it was a very strict religious school, one that didn't hesitate to kick kids out for seemingly small infractions. Dress codes were strictly enforced, chapel attendance was required, language rules were enforced, dating rules were enforced, and certain sorts of people weren't wanted.

The gay kids kept disappearing. The Evangel administrators seemed to be surprised that new ones showed up every fall. They remained fairly well-hidden; always behaving impeccably, blending in, and performing well just like the others. The non-gay students pretty well knew who was gay and who wasn't, though it wasn't talked about out loud. Oh, yes, there was the occasional rumor here and there, always followed by a tsk-tsk, a cocked eyebrow, and a reminder to pray for the wayward soul of the misdirected youth, but that was about it. And then they would disappear.

Some spent a semester – maybe two – and then were never seen again. Others had the misfortune of being "outed" to administrative officials and leaving in the middle of a term; or even worse yet, actually getting caught by college spies as they snuck into a local gay bar. Theirs was a bad lot; not only were they hauled before the administration, but their parents were called as well. There was no privacy for the victims. Two kids were even expelled two weeks before their graduation, not being allowed to finish their final exams, their diplomas withheld.

I stayed as far away as possible from anyone I suspected of being gay. I was on a mission to find a new life and I couldn't afford any mistakes. That degree was my ticket to the future, whatever it held.

I witnessed my first gay-bashing one day in the cafeteria at Evangel when Dan Mosedale, a gigantic basketball player, outed a little pipsqueak gay kid in the lunch line in front of the entire student body! It was terrible. Apparently, this kid had made a pass at Dan the day before. Dan reacted violently, the kid just barely escaping a severe beating, only now to be trapped in the lunch line, Dan ahead of him a ways, but all at once noticing him. Dan hollered out, "Hey, you little faggot! Why don't you tell everyone here that you're a fag! Tell them how you want to do it with me! Go ahead, you little pervert!

Let's see how brave you are now!"

No response. The kid hung his head and tried to disappear into the wall, a couple hundred surprised pairs of eyes staring at him. He must have weighed all of a hundred pounds.

"I'm talking to you, you homo!" Dan screamed. The room was absolutely quiet, everyone looking first at Dan, then at the kid.

Dan pushed his way through the line, back to the kid, leaning his hand against the wall, towering over him. "What's your problem, homo?" He shoved him. The kid tried to turn to walk away, but Dan grabbed him by the shoulders and slammed him against the wall. "I said, what's your problem, you stupid fag!"

"Leave him alone, Dan!" I hollered from the entrance of the cafeteria where I had been frozen, watching this horrible scene unfold. I wasn't much bigger than the runt kid, but my adrenaline was up from watching this monster prepare to beat the hell out of him, and I couldn't be quiet.

Dan spun around, glaring at me. "Why, are you one too?" he bellowed.

Dan was on my dorm floor. I saw him every day. He was a close friend of my roommate; he hung out in my room. He had a threatening personality normally, and his face was now twisted into a menacing, evil sneer. I glared right back, locking eyes. "I said leave him alone, Dan."

Other students, awakened from their stupors by my outburst, backed away, expecting a fight was about to erupt. Then little by little the crowd began murmuring, "Yeah, Dan, leave him alone!" "Pick on someone your own size, you brute!"

And then Dutch, my roommate, walked over to Dan,

grabbed him by the arm, and walked him away from the kid. "Leave him alone, Dan," he said quietly. Dan yelled at the boy a couple more times but allowed Dutch to take him to the head of the cafeteria line. Dutch was the only one who could have gotten away with that without being decked.

The kid left at the end of the semester.

But they kept coming; gay Christian kids that my church claimed didn't exist, or at least shouldn't exist. Gay kids of straight, God-fearing parents. They were everywhere and nowhere, trying to fit in; an invisible, shameful minority. Though these handsome, beautiful, smart, talented, kind, and funny kids mattered in the world, they were the scourge of the church. Slowly they were destroyed, bit by bit, one by one. It was the Evangelical Christian thing to do: breed, produce queer kids eight percent of the time, and then throw them all in the gutter, keeping only the straight ones.

And I just kept watching it all unfold, internalizing the message.

In spite of the downsides, I soon really found my way at Evangel, made a lot of friends, and had a fabulous and hilarious time of it. I learned a lot about people as I went along and discovered that I could not have been more naïve about life and society as a whole. I had to adjust very quickly. I watched and listened a lot, and said very little for a long time. And I began to change for the better, despite being surrounded by immoral Evangelical hypocrisy.

On one of my routine calls home from college that first year, Mom innocently told me that Kathy, now fourteen, was dating a twenty-one-year-old guy that I knew back home. I screamed.

"It's okay, David, I've got him going to church. Nothing will happen."

"Nothing will happen, MY ASS!" I hollered. "Just WHAT do you think this guy is thinking about every second of the day, Mom? Baking cookies? He'll have her pregnant before summer, mark my words! I don't care if he's going to church or not! He's a GUY, Mom. GUY equals SEX! Get him away from her! Do you hear me? Or I'm going to drive up there and chase him away myself!"

Dad got on the phone. "Now, David, I'm pretty sure things are fine. He seems like a pretty nice fella. I don't think any-thing'll happen."

"Dammit, you guys, how many pregnant daughters do you have to have before you get it? If she gets pregnant, I swear I'll throttle you both! Kath is the top student in her class! I want her to go to college and not ruin her life!"

"David," Mom replied, "I'll remind you that we're the par-ents; we know what we're doing. I'm sure things are just fine. You just do your studies and never mind. Besides, he's saved now."

"SAVED?! SO WHAT! Saved people have sex ALL THE TIME!"

That following summer, I went home and worked for Dad for no pay in order to assuage my guilt for leaving him. It was an absolute disaster.

School was always over early at Evangel, so I was home by early May. I slipped into my jeans, chambray shirt, and work boots with ease. They were clothes that were so attuned to my body from years of wear that they could have climbed onto me by themselves. It felt good to be home; I was ready to work.

I got up early and strode into the kitchen to grab a ba-nana or something, thinking I was up before Dad, but there he was at the kitchen table, ready to jump down my throat. "Why were you laying-around in bed so late? I guess I'm just going to sit around here for the next half hour, since you've already taken a break for the day. I may as well, too." He started swatting flies with a fly swatter while he chewed my ass for a while, then studiously ignored me. I asked him what we were doing for the day and where he wanted me to start, but he just snorted. "What did ya come home for? I don't need the likes of you around here; I've been getting along just fine without you! If Springfield is so great, why don't you just keep your worthless ass down there? Maybe stick your nose in some more worthless books! I can't believe you'd dare to show your worthless face around here." I finally got tired of his diatribe and decided to go outside and figure out what needed to be done and get started on my own. So, I did.

I pulled some tools out of the truck and started tinkering with one of the tractors that he'd told me the night before wasn't working quite right; I finished that job and pulled the chainsaw out of the pickup bed, preparing to cut down a dead tree beside the machine shed. Dad finally appeared, having had a leisurely breakfast, and started ripping on me again.

"What the hell are you doing? I didn't ask you to cut down that tree. Just put that chainsaw back; I don't even want you touching my stuff. You don't know a damn thing about what I need to be done around here."

"Dad, for heaven's sake! I asked you what needed to be done and you wouldn't tell me, so I'm just starting on the obvious. If you don't like what I'm doing, then tell me what you want me to work on instead! I'm here to work!"

"I don't want you working on ANYTHING around here!"

he spit.

I stared at him.

"Dad, what the hell is your problem?"

He glared at me murderously. "Why don't you just get the hell out of here and never come back! I don't want you around here anyway, now or ever! You *left!* So, just get the hell out of here once and for all! You don't want to be here and I don't want you here. Just LEAVE! Go! GET OUT!"

I froze. I knew he was hurt because I didn't want to farm. I knew he loved my brother more and missed him terribly. But – he didn't want me around *at all?* He'd just said it out loud, the thing I'd always feared was true.

I stared at him for a moment, then felt tears welling up from nowhere, spilling over my lashes in an unexpected gush, and I turned and ran as fast as I could to get away from him. I had to get away – I couldn't let him see me cry. I felt sick and thought I was going to throw up. I always thought Dad didn't think much of me, but for him to actually say it, and to say that he didn't want me, his own son, was absolutely devastating, and it cut to my core. The pain in my chest, the shortness of breath, the sobs – just came out of me from everywhere. I had been hurt a lot in my short life, but I didn't know an eighteen-year-old boy, a man, really, could cry or be hurt that badly by words.

I managed to run blindly to the chicken house and ducked inside, where I bawled out loud, a lifetime's worth of trauma and grief pouring out all at once. Suddenly Dad appeared at the door. He said nothing, but looked like he was about to cry. I turned away as he reached out to me, then brushed him aside as I ran out the door and up to the house. I was still only a kid, as it turned out, and I needed my dad. But not like this. If I had truly been a man by then, an adult, perhaps this encounter may have had a different, better ending.

Slamming the back door, I walked rapidly through the kitchen and living room, through the hallway with the green linoleum floor with all its wisps and patterns, and into my bedroom, where I shut the door quietly and sat on the side of the bunk bed. My sobs stopped. Shock and grief were gradually replaced with a cold, deadly rage. In a matter of minutes, my mind went through everything that ever happened between me and my dad, and a lot of it was ugly. Hadn't he said to me before my brother's body was even cold in the grave that I would have to take his place on the farm? Replace him, as if I had to be erased? Had he ever had any concern for what I wanted in my life? Had he ever told me "thank you" for anything, or "good job"? And what about those beatings? Had he ever been anything but confrontational and demeaning to me since I was the smallest of boys? Would he have wailed night after night if it had been me that died seven years ago, or would he have just been glad it wasn't his other son?

The door suddenly opened and there he stood, now crying himself.

"I didn't mean to say that, David." A sort of apology, the first he'd ever uttered.

I looked him squarely in the eyes, cold-hearted, murderous, and unafraid for the first time. I looked at him for a long moment, blue eyes staring into blue eyes, my young face a mirror of his old face, the face that represented what I was doomed to become if I didn't stand up for myself.

"Yes, you did, Dad. You've been waiting to say that for a long time. You can't come walking into my room now with tears in your eyes and take it back. You can NEVER take it back, Dad. Some things can't be undone, and there are some things *that even you can't fix,* and this is one of them. You son-of-a-bitch. You don't even know who I am! I'm not my brother! Now get the hell out of my room."

He stood there for a moment looking like he might say something, and then turned and walked away, leaving the door open. I sat there for a long time, thinking.

No money. No place to stay in town, no friends or social life here because that fucking farm had consumed my entire existence day in and day out until the day I left for college. Shit. Shit! Shit! Shit!

I was just stuck with no place to go. I sat a bit longer, got up, put on my cap, went outside to see what Dad was doing, found him working on the field cultivator, picked up a wrench and some new shovels that needed to be put on, and started to work without a word. It was a horrible day and a horrible week and a horrible summer with lots of tension and terse exchanges, with unspoken hurt on both sides. The incident was never talked about again. Mom knew something terrible had happened between Dad and me, but I only told her a little, wanting to spare her my pain. Like her, I had given up on my relationship with Dad. My fate was sealed, and I was determined to stay on my path of escape through education.

"Kathy, how far along are you?" I asked, as we walked quietly along the farm lane into the field. It was now only early June but it was already the longest summer of my life.

"I think about five months."

"Is it moving already?

"Yeah, it moves all the time."

"Does Scott know?"

"Yes."

"Does anyone else know?"

"No."

She didn't cry; her voice was steady.

"She's only fifteen and a half," I thought to myself. I looked at her from the corner of my eye. She was so pretty, and tough, too. Her lower abdomen was bulging quite a bit. I suspected it when I got home from college in May. How come only Nancy and I noticed? How dumb can people be?

"I think you should get an abortion," I said matter-of-factly. "This baby is going to ruin your life, Kathy. You're too little and too young to even have it."

"I can't," she responded. "I would hate myself for the rest of my life."

"What about adoption then?"

"No, I can't do that either. It's my baby, and I'm keeping it."

I sighed. "We better go and tell Mom then. They need to know, and she'll have to help. I don't want to tell Dad, knowing his temper. Maybe Mom can tell him. You can't quit school, Kath. You're too damned smart. You need to finish. And you shouldn't get married either, that would be so stupid. You're not ready for any of this. Just have the baby and stay in school and don't make any other decisions for now, okay? Promise me..."

"Okay."

DARTH VADER

The spring of that awful summer, my sister Julie decided to raise some exotic chickens. She had all types – Golden Polish, Bantams, Cochins, you name it. There was one little Polish rooster she was particularly attached to whom she named Darth Vader due to the "helmet" of black feathers adorning his skull. Little Darth was treated to lots of special treatment, including naps in Julie's lap, ice cream sandwiches, jaunts through the living room, and rides in the car and on the bike. Thus, Darth grew up to be somewhat of a spoiled brat of a rooster with a weird psychological overlay, not knowing for sure whether he was a rooster or a person. He was generally charming and handsome, topknot and gold-and-black breeding plumage oiled to a perfect sheen, but he could be an asshole.

Darth Vader began to look suspiciously upon three-year-old Joey as some sort of male competitor in his little world of chickens and men. It was subtle at first, an occasional glare from behind a tree as little Joey sauntered out to play, but then gradually overt, stalking directly behind him with neck feathers puffed up in a rage, dancing around in the dust with wings down and spurs displayed menacingly in the sunlight, eventually sidling right up to him in direct confrontation.

At first, Joey thought it quite funny, this rooster following him around, but as Darth's feints got closer and closer, he began to get concerned and skittish, looking carefully out the back door before darting out to play, hoping Darth wouldn't be in a bad mood, sharpening his spurs.

Well, it had to happen, I suppose. Joey's fear got the best of him one day and he made the mistake of running away from one of Darth's fake attacks, giving Darth the impression that he could take his little competitor and whip him. The result was predictable; every time Joey left the house, Darth would be waiting for him. No matter where he was, he'd see Joey and take off after him, murder in his eyes, flapping wildly, leaping, and stabbing at Joey's little legs as he ran screaming and crying into the house.

Even at three, Joey was a lot bigger than a chicken. None of us understood why he didn't just kick the hell out of little Darth when he attacked. Heck, I drop-kicked Darth a good twenty-five feet one day when he decided to take me on. He came back for a second helping, but after being kicked twenty-five feet twice, he thought better of it from then on. I calmly suggested to Joey he do the same thing, but his feeble kicks didn't faze Darth much and the chicken would always win.

Dad, of course, found the entire matter ridiculous. How could a kid, even at three, allow himself to be beaten up by a chicken? I mean, for heaven's sake! It was just a little three-pound chicken; Joey could have picked it up and wrung its neck if he wanted to. What sort of a wimp was he?

"Good grief, Joe, can't you even beat up a chicken??!!" he hollered at him one day, as Joey came bawling in the back door, chicken-whipped for the hundredth time. "I'll have to make ya a big stick so you can beat up a tiny little chicken, I suppose. This is the dumbest thing I've ever heard of!"

So, he went outside and cut a branch off an elm tree, turning it into a club for Joey, who kept it by the back door so he could bonk Darth Vader on the head any time he came near. Eventually, Darth recognized the significance of the club swinging in Joey's little hands and kept his distance. He strutted and glared, though. If Joey turned his back for even a second, he'd be on him in a flash, getting in at least one good lick before Joey could whack him with the club. Little Darth, just like the real Darth Vader, always came back.

It was about this time, one sunny afternoon, that Joey decided to catch a duck. He sauntered out the back door with his big stick, looking this way and that for Darth. It was a hot day, and Darth was dusting himself under a shrub with his little harem, so Joey went on about his mission. He found the ducks in the driveway by a puddle and took off after them, trying to find the slowest one to catch. They fluttered about, quacking and squawking, until one of the young drakes got separated and ran out around the windmill, where Joey caught up with it and cornered it by a silage wagon that was in repair mode with all of its wheels removed temporarily. Joey crept forward to grab him, so the duck did the only thing he could and dove head first into the tiny space under the wagon. Joey, not to be outdone, dove right in after him.

A while later, I got up from my half-hour summer afternoon nap to go out and find something to do. I got a big drink of water and headed out the back, the screen door banging as Mom hollered after me to see what Joey was up to.

"He went outside quite a while ago! See if you can find him!"

Yawning, I walked out toward the windmill. Man, it was sure hot. I kicked up the dust and noticed Darth and his tribe panting under the bushes. "Too hot even for Darth," I thought. Ambling on, I stopped suddenly, hearing a strange muffled sound. I listened intently. It sounded like a little kid crying, but almost like it was underground. I listened long enough to get the general direction, then darted under the windmill and stopped to listen. I heard it again, but now louder. It was very close. I walked around the silage wagon and...there was the bottom half of Joey sticking out from under the edge of the wagon.

"Oh fuck!" I thought as I leaped down by his legs and strained my neck to see under the wagon. "Oh fuck, this fucking wagon is smashing Joey's head...oh my god..."

The adrenaline rush was magic potion in my veins. Every muscle in my body began to vibrate with energy, and everything around me vanished as I focused on Joey.

I ripped out the grass and weeds beside him, yanking big bunches of dirt out of the parched earth, making a space big enough for me to force my head and torso under the wagon. It took only a second. I had to get him out. I heaved the wagon up enough to squeeze in. I could see his body and...where was his head?

"Joey!" I yelled.

Joey let out a loud crying wail. "I'm caught! My head is caught!"

I forced my way in farther, the adrenaline giving me unimaginable strength. I craned my neck around to see that indeed, Joey's head was caught between a supporting I-beam and the bottom of the wagon, a space just large enough to allow him to have forcefully pushed his head through, but not large enough to get it back out. "Can you breathe okay Joey?" I asked frantically. "Yeah, I can breathe...but my head is stuck under here and it won't come out," he wailed. "Are you hurt?" I asked. "No, I'm not hurt. I just can't get out. I chased a duck in here and it went through here and I thought I could get through too, but I got stuck! You gotta get me out David! Help me!"

I wiggled my arms around his chest and up to his neck and felt around. He was really wedged in tight. I got ahold of the base of his skull and slowly twisted this way and that, pulling with moderate force, but his ears got caught on the sharp edges of the I-beam and he screamed in pain. He was really wedged in there.

"Joey, I'm going to go and get some more help. I can't get you out of here by myself. You have to be okay to just rest here until I get back. Don't cry. It'll be okay. The wagon won't fall on you. Just be really still. I'll be right back, okay? I'll only be a minute." "Okay," he replied tearfully. "But hurry up, I'm scared."

I squeezed my arms back down to my sides, wiggled myself out a ways, pushed with all of my might to get the wagon off my chest, hooked my feet on the ground and pulled myself out from under the wagon. I turned and patted Joey's legs and said, "I'll be right back," and then took off for the house.

I slammed the back door with a bang, hollering for Mom, who leaped up and was out the door in a flash, having to see for herself that her littlest son was still alive after the story I'd rapidly reported. I caught up with her in a second, the other kids appearing at our sides, all assessing the situation. In a hurry, Mom decided we had to get more help so she ran to the house and called the fire department in New Sharon. They appeared in a matter of minutes, along with an ambulance and flashing lights. Soon the area was crawling with uniformed men trying to figure out how to get Joey unstuck. They quickly dug out more space under him with a spade so they could get around him, and two at a time from each side, they tried to work his head out of the crevice, but all to no avail. There was debate about jacking the wagon up, but they were afraid it would torque his neck, so that idea was thrown out. How about cutting the I-beam with a chainsaw? No, too noisy and dangerous right there by his head...but there had to be a way.

One of the ambulance crew walked over with a big jar of Vaseline. "Here, lube his head and ears up with this and see if you can squeeze him through that way." So, his head was promptly encased in Vaseline, and by tilting his head way forward, they managed to get his ears over the edge of the I-beam, and then slowly pried his head through until it came out with a pop.

Mom grabbed his legs and pulled him out from under the wagon and sat holding him as the firemen extricated themselves.

About then, Nancy came home from a shopping trip, only to see firetrucks and an ambulance in the driveway, lights flashing, and immediately assumed one of her brothers or sisters was killed again. She skidded to a halt in the driveway and ran in hysterics to the scene, expecting the worst, but finding only a Vaseline-headed boy surrounded by rescue workers and the rest of us all covered with dirt and sweat. Joey was still crying a little, but now was embarrassed by the crowd and just wanted to go to the house, where Mom was happy to take him.

We thanked the ambulance crew and firefighters profusely. They were quiet. Several of them still remembered coming out on another hot summer day seven years before to load up that Coster boy who hadn't fared so well.

Kathy gave birth that fall of 1979 to a retarded baby named Travis. He had a severe case of Down syndrome, combined with other brain-development problems. The birth itself was unremarkable. The baby, however, was a disaster, and would never be able to function as a person.

The next spring, home from college, I was visiting with Kath in her room, talking about her future plans, how she was getting along, and so forth. She fed the baby as we talked, then got up and laid him on the bed. I was just sick about her chances of having a decent future; the baby was only going to be a bigger problem as he got older; he was seriously disabled. She was holding her own, though, doing better than I expect most anyone else would do at her age.

We chatted away for a few minutes, when I glanced over at the baby sleeping quietly on the bed.

Wait a minute; something was wrong. His color looked off. I stood up and walked over to the bed, peering at the baby for a few seconds.

"Kathy, something's wrong with this baby. I don't think it's breathing. It looks like it's dead."

Indeed, the baby was blue-gray, lips purplish, and it wasn't breathing.

I felt a flood of relief. Suddenly, there was a silver lining on the cloud of Kathy's life; this terrible burden had been lifted; lifted by a fortuitous and unexpected event, terrible though it may appear, but lifted nonetheless. A gift. How rapidly one's thoughts fly in such situations! My initial reaction had been to reach for the baby, but then, I hesitated; don't do anything; just wait a few seconds longer and it will all be over. Whatever is happening can't take long. The baby was either dead or almost dead.

And then Kathy uttered the most pitiful, shrill, anguished cry I have ever heard, the sound of a mother losing her baby, a deep, guttural, keening coming from someplace I couldn't know. It went through me like a dagger.

My reverie ended. I snatched Travis up by the feet, flipped him upside down and whacked him hard over and over on the back. I put him back on the bed, ready to give him mouth-to-mouth. I didn't know what I was doing. How do you do CPR on a baby? I surely didn't know, but I was about to figure it out. I glared at the baby and shook him. Kathy let out another cry of anguish, and just then, he gasped. I smacked him again, and he gasped again, and then again. His color came back; he moved and started to bawl. Kathy swept him up and ran to the living room, hollering for Mom. The two of them jumped in the car and drove to the hospital, where the doctors found nothing wrong. Maybe his tongue just blocked his airway; Down syndrome babies have trouble with their big tongues when lying on their backs.

So, he survived. And life got very hard for Kath.

"What do you mean his head is stuck? How can a baby's head be stuck in a C-section? Jesus Christ, just pull him out!" I yelled over the drapes at the two obstetricians struggling to deliver my gigantic son through a too-small incision.

Julie had been in labor for thirty-six hours with no progress whatsoever, and now our first son was in trouble. What started out as fun and exciting was now threatening as hell. Julie looked up at me from her point of crucifixion on the operating table, surprised at my outburst. She was exhausted but as usual organized and even-tempered, even with a giant baby being yanked out through a hole in her belly.

"I'm not kidding," I yelled again. "I'll come over there and pull him out myself if you don't do it RIGHT NOW!"

I'm afraid I was one of those fathers who should have been left in the waiting room. Truth is, though, I actually could have gone around and pulled him out myself, having already done it a number of times by then as a medical student.

Somehow, his head finally flew out with a distinct "thwonk," then abruptly turned and looked right at me, eyes wide open. I sucked in my breath. "Oh my god it's me! Shit, Julie, I'm not kidding, it's me! An exact replica! Get him out! Get him all the way out!"

To this day, I don't quite know what got into me that afternoon; perhaps a residual demon from Rosemary's Baby? I hadn't been very nice, but then considering my experience with trapped and bashed-in heads, well, what do you expect. I just wanted my little baby out.

We named him Adam, Man of Red Earth. Born in Oklahoma where the dirt is so red it hurts your eyes. Everyone survived, but Julie got as sick as hell with septic shock, and things were nip and tuck there for a while. It's the way it goes. Every day we're alive is largely just dumb luck, though on occasion it's the antibiotics.

ACCEPTANCE ───────────────

I struggled with the hemostat, sweating under my mask, trying to work the tip around the cystic duct, studying the tis-
sues for the tell-tale trace of the cystic artery finding its way
onto the gall bladder wall. Dr. Mouw watched me work, saying nothing, assisting me and occasionally studying my face.

"What is wrong with me?" I yelled at myself in my brain.
"I am so fucking stupid. I can't even do a simple little thing
like this, can't even take out a stupid gall bladder, for God's
sake. I can't believe how dumb..." And then I stopped dead
in my tracks. My hands froze. I stared at the liver and gall
bladder. Everything around me vanished, and I was suddenly in a soundless tunnel as realization flooded over me. Dad
was nowhere around, yet there he was in my head, that old
tape recording of him, trapped in my brain, telling me how
utterly incapable I was. I was still letting him hold me back,
letting him defeat me still. But no, wait! I was twenty-seven
years old! Why was I allowing this nonsense to continue? Why
wasn't I saying "No!" when the tape recording played? Why
wasn't I making a new recording that said "I can" instead of
"I can't"?

It hit me like a load of bricks. I had become my own worst
enemy. Where Dad had left off, I had started in all over again.
This was my demon. I had internalized all the negativity, and
it kept coming back to haunt me. It had to stop. I had to put

it behind me once and for all. I had to "kill the father" if I expected to become the man I wanted to be.

Dr. Mouw looked at me. "Are you going to finish this operation anytime today, Dave?"

"Yes," I replied, coming out of my tunnel. I popped the tip of the hemostat into precisely the proper place, freeing up the artery, and laying out the structures as if they were a picture in an anatomy book. I paused then, and was quiet for a moment. "I'll be finishing this operation today, and every day going forward, and perfectly every time."

Things were seriously different after that. I steadily beat back the negative influence of my father, day by day, case by case. And not just at work, but at home as well, nurturing my little sons, encouraging my beautiful and talented wife, and working extra hard as a father and husband. When I didn't know how to be the dad, I mentally placed myself back in time to see what I needed from Dad that I didn't get when I was two, three, four, five, sixteen, and so on; if I still wasn't sure, I just did the opposite of whatever he had done. Most of all, I treated everyone in my little family with love, respect, and fairness, and we talked all the time about everything under the sun. Gradually, I undid the damage to myself while making an optimal world for my own boys. It wasn't as hard as one might think; mostly I just loved them and always made sure they knew it; and then I respected them and talked to them as if they were sensible and intelligent adults; and that's what they then became.

By the time I was thirty-three, I could finally look at my father without malice and appreciate the gifts he gave me — my life, my inquisitiveness, my unusual personality, my persistence, and yes, even my difficult childhood. He did his best,

I figured. As his son, there came a point when it just wasn't dignified to blame him for any of my travails or personal difficulties. I had, after all, pulled the remaining splinter of his presence right out of my head. I mostly forgave him, and that was ultimately the key to letting it all go and becoming no longer a boy, but a man. The key to being a father, though, was remembering and relearning how to be a boy again, and it took my three little sons to teach me that.

UNEXPLAINABLE THINGS ─────────────

On June 8th, 1998, my thirty-eighth birthday, I tossed my clothes into the back of my pickup and moved to town. I left everything else with Julie and started completely over in a tiny apartment. The move had been scheduled for later that month, but as it grew closer and closer, neither of us could stand the stress of waiting and I just had to leave. It was such a relief. I slept like a stone for the next six months; hard, dreamless sleep like I'd never had in my life. I was sad, but my relief at being released exceeded all other emotion. I had felt the cold hard brick at the bottom of the well of depression, and I never wanted to go there again.

The boys came to town and stayed with me as they liked. We had made a very loose parenting plan for the boys. The process was transparent and based upon what they needed, not necessarily what Julie and I wanted for ourselves. The kids came first.

Over the next few months, I "came out" (I hate this term) to my siblings one at a time. I couldn't stand the idea of trying to explain my situation to all of them at once. Their reactions were mixed, but decidedly not bad. At the end of every conversation though, they each and every one said, "Whatever you do, don't tell Dad! It will kill him!" I thought it was a ridiculous remonstration, as if this particular thing – of all the hardships Dad had in his life – would be the thing that actually pushed him over the edge into oblivion. For Christ's sake!

I told the boys that August. They were just eight, eleven, and twelve. I was making spaghetti and had just served up three big plates for them as they sat around the tiny table in my apartment, when Seth said, "Dad, when are you ever going to tell us why you had to leave? It doesn't seem like anything is even wrong with you and Mom, and none of this makes any sense! Why don't you just come back home?"

So, I was compelled by surprise to tell them then and there, even though I didn't feel quite ready. I just blurted it out. "I'm gay." They all looked at me for a second. I was afraid of their response; afraid they wouldn't want me anymore. I waited. And then, finally: "Is that all?" Seth said incredulously. "Good grief, Dad, I thought it was something BAD! I see now! Of course, you can't come home!"

"I thought it was something bad too," Adam said. "This doesn't even matter. You're not leaving, are you? Just don't leave. That's all that matters." This may have been the wisest thing ever said by a twelve-year-old, and looking back on it now, I realize it undid the scar of my father telling me he "didn't want me around here" on that horrible day in the summer of 1979. My kids wanted me around no matter what. They loved me regardless. I had been terrified to tell them my truth for no reason. It was the biggest relief of my life.

"You guys are apparently a lot smarter than I am," I said in wonder. "Now let's eat some spaghetti! It's good!"

I finally got around to Mom in September of 1998, the last on my list except for Dad. She actually argued with me when

I told her I was gay. "Oh, you are not!" she stated emphatically. It was the most asinine of all the responses I'd received. And then she started in with, "You know the Bible says..." at which point I stopped her and told her exactly what I was going to do with that Bible if she didn't shut the hell up, for once in her life, about that goddamned book. "Your Bible, that church, and your religious beliefs did more harm to me than you can ever imagine, Mom! For once in your life, stop thinking about religion and LOOK at me! SEE me for who I am! You don't even know me! As usual, all you care about is your faith, regardless of the harm it's done!"

This was not very nice, but it snapped her out of her religious reverie, and she finally knocked off the Bible talk and listened. When I was finished, she said that in retrospect she probably should have known all along, and she was sorry it hadn't ever crossed her mind, but it just wasn't something that was ever discussed in those days. "No shit," I replied. And then she said, "Whatever you do, don't tell your dad. I'm sure it will kill him."

"I'll tell him if I want," I said. "If it kills him, then too bad. He damned near killed *me* enough times over the years, so it'll just serve him right. Maybe he'll finally *understand* a few things."

I didn't tell him just then. I decided I would wait for the right moment.

But then, in January, Mom went off to town for breakfast, leaving Dad to fend for himself as he puttered around the house. Having realized she'd forgotten something when she got a mile down the road, she turned around and went home to pick it up, only to find Dad slumped over the kitchen table, unconscious.

She called an ambulance, then called me at the hospital where I worked in Grinnell. I reassured her, and soon met them in the ER. Dad was out of it. He'd clearly had a big stroke, probably the most devastating thing that could happen to him, knowing his personality and aversion to the idea of being "crippled up" as he liked to call it.

Mom and I had an intense discussion with Dr. Anderson, the internist, after Dad's CT scan showed diffuse involvement of one entire hemisphere of his brain. He was clearly in serious trouble. There was a remote possibility that TPA, the new clot-busting drug, might break up the clot and save at least most of the brain tissue without leaving him with any serious disability. It had, after all, been only about a half-hour since the stroke, and brains can heal if the arterial blockage can be remedied soon enough. It was a very difficult decision, but I allowed the treatment, thinking all along that Dad would kill me if it didn't work properly and he ended up being alive but disabled.

The TPA was given, and within thirty minutes, he suddenly woke up and sat up on his gurney. "WHAT did you DO? Where am I? What's going on?" He looked at me for a moment. "What have you done?" he repeated. "I was dead. Gone! Why did you bring me back? I don't want to be here. Let me go!" he yelled at me in complete disgust. "I was in a GOOD PLACE! I had my hands on the handles of the gates of heaven, and I was just about to open the door!"

Dad was a lot of things, but he wasn't ever a liar. So once again, I found myself looking into a pair of blue eyes and thinking to myself, as if I were once again three years old, "What is dead, anyway? What is death? What makes the body stop working, like a clock unwinding? When does the transition happen? And then what happens? It's not implausible that our essence somehow escapes and sails back into the universe, is it? We are, after all, just made of stardust. We are not just *in* the universe; we are *made* of it. Dad wasn't the first patient I knew who had some sort of a sense of an encounter with something else before being brought back from the brink of death. There are entire books about this. We don't know everything there is to know.

But, regardless, I'd made the wrong choice. If Dad lived, I would never hear the end of how I'd ruined his life by keeping him from dying. I imagined the endless stream of sarcasm he'd thrust on me until he got another chance to get to wherever it had been that he went while his brain wasn't working. My mind flew back to all those withering comments I'd received from him over the years. I didn't know whether to laugh or cry. The stroke had missed his speech center, so I was doomed to be tortured for the rest of his life.

For the next two hours in intensive care he complained bitterly about being "brought back," but then the blood thinners failed, his stroke reoccurred, and this time he got what he wanted.

Phone calls were made, and the kids came from all corners, streaming into the hospital along with their spouses or significant others, plus grandkids, plus friends – a lot of people.

We all came together at this moment in time, our thoughts focused on Mom and Dad. It's hard to get ten people on the same page when end-of-life issues arise. For most there was no question that we'd leave him be and let him go with no further intervention, though Ev struggled with the decision more than the others. She told me many years later that she thought I had killed him in a way by not advocating to try to save him those last few days. I guess it just didn't register for her that it didn't matter what was done for medical care at that point, as the die was cast and the outcome was certain. For four days we sat by his bedside talking and remembering, laughing and crying, putting it all in perspective, trying to forgive more, and growing up a little more.

My sister Julie was the last to arrive. During the three days it took her to get there, Dad remained comatose and unresponsive. We talked to him, massaged his limbs and back, applied lotion, and moved him frequently. He developed an infection with high fevers. We gave him comfort only, knowing he'd want nothing else. When Julie finally arrived, she went straight to his side. All the rest of us had been in and out, knowing he was comatose and unresponsive. Julie hadn't seen him for a long time; we all felt badly about that; no opportunity to say goodbye, we thought. Julie touched Dad on the shoulder and said, "Dad, I'm here finally. It's Julie."

To our astonishment, he immediately reached up with his non-paralyzed hand and, without opening his eyes, placed it squarely on top of her head, touching her hair and making a sound. Julie grasped his hand and held it for a bit until the strength went out of it again. And that was the last meaningful thing Dad did. To this day I don't understand it, but cannot discount that, somehow, he couldn't let go until the last of his children got to say goodbye.

But that still was not quite the end. I was exhausted. I continued to work during the four days that Dad was in the hospital, checking on him between my surgeries, sitting with him when I could, comforting other families in the hospital that were struggling with their own loved ones, doing what I do best. It kept me even to be working, and it kept me comfortable to know Dad was in my hospital.

The day that Julie arrived would be Dad's last, and I knew it. I had been through this too many times with other families in other situations. I told Mom when I left that evening that Dad wouldn't live through the night. Some of the other kids went home, some stayed. And, of course, Mom stayed. I went on home to try to get some rest, knowing I would be called back in later when he passed.

And so, in my apartment, I slept – a very heavy, deep, hard sleep that exhaustion brings.

Suddenly, Dad was in my dreams, laughing and whizzing around in my head, a happy streak of light. Or *was* it a dream? "I'm free! I'm free!" he crowed ecstatically. It seemed like he was right there. An unspoken stream of his consciousness seemed to be pouring in, blending with my own consciousness from a thousand directions at once. I saw everything he had ever known and felt in his life as if we had a mind meld. Suddenly, I understood him, and he understood me – all of me. I felt it, a bi-directional exchange of our minds. It all happened in a split second.

With a tap on the back of my head, like he used to do when I was a little kid, he awakened me – and then zoomed off like a shooting star, happy as a lark. I could see him flying away into the universe, a tiny bright comet, just as my eyes opened. The last thing he said, as he flew off, was, "I have to find Neal!"

It was 1:02 a.m. on the alarm clock, the room black and silent.

I sat up on the side of the bed. That couldn't have been real, could it? It *felt* real. I was sure Dad was just here in my room. I was shocked. I reached for the phone to call the hospital, but it rang in my hand before I could even pick up. I lifted the receiver in mid-ring, and answered, "Hello."

"Dr. Coster, this is the nurse from the hospital. I'm sorry to tell you this, but your dad just passed away a minute ago."

I didn't say anything for a few seconds.

"I know," I replied. "He was just here."

I slowly got dressed, thinking. I felt really weird, almost exhilarated. I went out to the pickup. The parking lot was dark. I drove the few blocks to the hospital, strode through the doors, and took the stairs two at a time. The night nurses greeted me with sympathy when I reached the desk and then watched me as a group as I walked down the hall, alone.

"Are you okay?" one of them offered from behind me.

"I'm okay," I said.

I turned back to them. They looked at me, uncertain.

"Seriously, I'm absolutely fine." I smiled at them all, and paused a moment.

"Actually, I'm even better than fine. Thanks for asking."

And of course, I was.

POSTSCRIPT ———————————

Our youngest son, Sam, lived, even though there seemed to be no hope with the type of Stage 4 B-Cell lymphoma he had. He had brilliant doctors at the Siteman Cancer Center in St. Louis who were willing to try a new technique out of Stanford University to try to save him, though they first had to prove the tumor wasn't carrying a lethal gene that defies all treatment, and then had to prove that the cancer wasn't also in his spinal canal or brain. Awaiting the test results that would determine whether he had any chance at all was just awful. When we got the news that he didn't have the lethal gene, and that there was no evidence of tumor cells in his central nervous system, we all just collapsed. There was a very tiny ray of hope, after all. At twenty-three, he was incredibly strong, both physically and mentally. We were filled with dread, but cautiously optimistic.

It was a long and difficult road for treatment and recovery: two and a half years of chemo, radiation, immunotherapy, and two stem cell transplants. It took a toll on all of us, but especially, of course, Sam. He really suffered, especially when the cancer returned a few months after completion of his first course of treatment. But they knocked the cancer back again, this time with a highly toxic potion with the acronym "BEAM." BEAM kills every cell that happens to be growing and dividing, healthy or not, so cancer cells, which are always dividing, are killed along with many dividing healthy cells. It brings the person to the brink of death because the whole body is poisoned, and they get extremely sick. There is a high risk of infection and sepsis during this time, as the patient's bone marrow is wiped out and they cannot develop an immune response to an infection; there are no white blood cells remaining to protect them. The poison must be strong enough to infiltrate every cell space of the body and affect every actively dividing cell. If even one cancer cell gets away, the cancer will come back; so the poison doses must be very high.

Before giving BEAM, the doctors extracted some of Sam's healthy stem cells, cells which are always circulating in the blood, cells that could "rescue" him from the effects of BEAM. These cells are pluripotent – they are like embryonic cells which will mature to adult cells when they land in an organ space. They can be frozen in liquid nitrogen, then thawed, and given back to the patient through an IV. Once back inside the body, the stem cells implant in the bone marrow space previously wiped out by BEAM, and recreate the patient's own bone marrow. The bone marrow rapidly begins producing all sorts of blood cells, including the white blood cells that are needed to fight off infection. This marrow development period is critical, and if any complications occur the patient won't make it. Luckily, all went smoothly.

Two months later, Sam was once again strong enough for the final step. The doctors once again treated him with BEAM to wipe out any cancer cells that might have gotten away, and then rescued him again, this time with a perfectly matched donor stem cell transplant, stem cells harvested from a living person who had donated them to help Sam, stem cells which, once mature, would also recognize Sam's cancer as an enemy and constantly survey his body for cancer cells, killing any upon discovery.

Once his new donor stem cells took hold and his marrow started working again, there was real hope, and little by little he grew stronger and stronger, and his tests kept coming back clear. The new bone marrow was doing its job. Nevertheless, we held our collective breath for ten years after, with a mix of fear and hope that Sam's new immune system would continue to do its magic.

Today, Sam is a game artist and public relations man for Butterscotch Shenanigans, a gaming company started by our middle son, Seth. Seth has a background in business and finance from the University of Northern Iowa and left the University of Iowa Law School to start the company. He is a master programmer and a savvy businessman. Adam attended the University of Chicago and then the University of Texas Southwestern for a PhD in molecular genetics. He left his research position there after obtaining the PhD and joined the other two boys at Butterscotch Shenanigans as their security expert and designer of programs to solve special problems. All the boys are married to wonderful women whom they met in college – Diana, Sampada, and Jenny (married respectively to Sam, Seth, and Adam), who have careers and expertise in art, tennis, business, writing, and medicine. They are very strong women who embody the power of the ideal American woman. They've all had complicated lives, which like mine, have informed the strength of their inner selves. They have all brought new meaning and perspective to my life. And most recently, Diana and Sam, through the miracle of reproductive technology, have had a baby. It's a new happy chapter to a story that needed a happy ending. We are all smiles.

My former wife, Julie, a highly talented nurse, became a medical-clinic organizer for two large corporations before moving on to do the same work with a large health insurance company. She has retired and moved to the East Coast with her current husband and remains well-connected with our boys, their spouses, and our new grandbaby. I can say nothing more than that, as the story of her life is her own to tell.

My mother, Eleanor, is eighty-eight and still out on the farm. She, I think, loves her life as a single person, surrounded by a ridiculous number of grandchildren and great-grandchildren. She's a tough lady and a survivor. She went back to college at age fifty-four and completed a four-year liberal arts degree with a major in Theology. She then became a minister until she got so old she couldn't do it anymore. She demonstrates an inner peace of surprising depth in her everyday life. She did the best she could for herself and with us, considering her circumstances, and that's all one can ask.

The rest of the siblings have all struggled with a variety of issues related to the complications of our upbringing. At the end of the day, we are all tackling the vicissitudes of life with courage, and we all found a path in life – even if it took longer than it should have.

As for me, I am once again married. My partner/husband of twenty-three years is Kevin Kopelson. He's a Jewish New Yorker, a highly educated fellow who attended The Juilliard School, Yale University, and Columbia Law. He practiced law in New York City for several years, then got a PhD in English from Brown University, and then became a professor and author at the University of Iowa. We were introduced by friends at age forty, and that was that. He changed my life and helped me become a person of the world by further stretching my boundaries and assumptions about people and cultures. He jumped right in as a mentor to the boys. He, Julie, and I co-parented them through junior high and high school, and then advised them as they found their way through college, higher education, and career choices. With his educational background, Kevin was a tremendous added resource for the boys. His childhood and cultural background could hardly be more dissonant to mine. We are very different people, but those differences have enhanced our relationship, our lives together, and our sons' growth. The summation of that entire life experience is a thing of consequence.

My thirty-one-year career as a surgeon in a rural hospital was highly satisfying, if not extremely difficult. I helped a lot of people and did a lot of great work, developing a reputation that brought patients to me from as far away as Europe. It turned out I was unusually capable as a surgeon, a fact that made it possible to have a very positive impact on my hospital and community, as well as on surgeons, residents, and med students who came to me to be mentored. The driving force in my career was the tragedies of my youth, I am sure, and those tragedies, along with the difficulties, allowed me to be a surgeon who could connect with his patients. Ultimately, technical skills aside, the ability to make those human connections drove the success of my career. A real doctor is a humanitarian, a person who resists passing judgment on the circumstances of his patients' lives. That doctor has torn himself down and put himself back together again, discarding the indoctrination of his youth and reinventing himself as a man of the world. This is no easy task, but it's necessary, not only to be an exceptional surgeon but to be an exceptional human. Regardless of one's path in life, striving always to be a better, kinder, more compassionate being is the path to satisfaction and peace.

The story of a life lived is always a story of both life and death, no matter who is telling the story, as we live and die all our lives in little waves. We die a little everytime we engage with social, cultural, mental, and economic trauma. We die a little everytime we suffer grief or physical trauma. But then we rebound to live life a little more. Back and forth, back and forth we go. Moments of true peace are few and far between, so when they occur we must take notice. We must choose life while we have it, and fight for it when it's worth living, no matter the difficulty. When physical death then finally comes, we know its okay.

Other things I've learned along the way:

Every child needs parents who truly see them and who respect each other.

As a person with a soul, a child does not need a church or religion. But if their parents insist on it, the child needs a church where all people are respected and treated kindly. Religion should be free of judgment and persecution of those who "don't fit in." If it can't be that, then it shouldn't be at all.

As citizens, we all need a government that recognizes that we all must be free to live our lives without demeaning constraints, a government that truly supports the concept of life, liberty, and the pursuit of happiness. We all need a society that does not harass and condemn, a society that is not racist, sexist, xenophobic, ableist, or homophobic.

As fathers, we all need different things. In my own case, I needed a mentor, but my own father was not it. I had to find other father figures upon whom to model my own fatherhood, and I needed enough emotional intelligence to undo the damage of my own difficult father-son relationship.

In our American culture, we have not, as a people, come close to the sort of humanity we should be performing for each other every day, whether that be in our families, or our churches, or society as a whole. We have made some progress, but we must do better.

If you are a person who has been abused in one way or another, you know it's more complicated than it might appear to an outsider. There can be more than one truth happening at once. For example: Yes, my dad is beating me and emotionally abusing me, and yes, I love him. Yes, my mom is being neglectful, and yes, *she* is being neglected. Sometimes, doing the best one can do in bad circumstances simply has to be good enough, whether it really is or not, and the consequences must be dealt with later, once we've escaped.

In life, we are all victims. We share this commonality. It's necessary to be able to talk about it so as to weaken it, not to empower it. Victimhood shouldn't become the thing we build our lives around. It's not a foundation of strength. At some point we must move on. We must see beyond it if we truly intend to live a satisfactory life. We must learn a better way of existing. We must decide to focus on what's good in life. We must decide to be good ourselves.

ACKNOWLEDGMENTS

Even So started twenty-five years ago as a collection of entertaining stories for my sons, stories meant to give context for them about who I am today. My husband, Kevin Kopelson read them too, and being an English professor handed them back and said, "David, these should be a memoir, not just a bunch of stories. You can make them into a book, and you should." His encouragement and support were always there, even when the project sat idle for a few years. His patient proofreading through the final stage of writing *Even So* was critical and added the polish that the book deserved.

I would also like to thank our little dog, Jocko Coster, our companion of nearly fifteen years. He sat at my feet under my desk every time I worked on my book. At night, though, he was secretly slipping away from our bed to write his own memoir with his own little paws on Kev's computer up in the attic. That book, *The Gay and Wondrous Life of Jocko Coster*, is a special book written for our granddaughter, Maeva Dove, and any other grandchildren we may someday have. It's full of love and magic and dreams, much like all our lives should be.

The Ice Cube Press began publishing in 1991 to focus on how to live with the natural world and to better understand how people can best live together in the communities they share and inhabit. Using the literary arts to explore life and experiences in the heartland of the United States we have been recognized by a number of well-known writers including: Bill Bradley, Gary Snyder, Gene Logsdon, Wes Jackson, Patricia Hampl, Greg Brown, Jim Harrison, Annie Dillard, Ken Burns, Roz Chast, Jane Hamilton, Daniel Menaker, Kathleen Norris, Janisse Ray, Craig Lesley, Alison Deming, Harriet Lerner, Richard Lynn Stegner, Richard Rhodes, Michael Pollan, David Abram, David Orr, and Barry Lopez. We've published a number of well-known authors including: Mary Swander, Jim Heynen, Mary Pipher, Bill Holm, Connie Mutel, John T. Price, Carol Bly, Marvin Bell, Debra Marquart, Ted Kooser, Stephanie Mills, Bill McKibben, Craig Lesley, Elizabeth McCracken, Derrick Jensen, Dean Bakopoulos, Rick Bass, Linda Hogan, Pam Houston, and Paul Gruchow. Check out Ice Cube Press books on our web site, join our email list, Facebook group, or follow us on Twitter. Visit booksellers, museum shops, or any place you can find good books and support our truly honest to goodness independent publishing projects and discover why we continue striving to hear the other side.

Ice Cube Press, LLC (Est. 1991)
North Liberty, Iowa, Midwest, USA

Resting above the Silurian and Jordan aquifers
steve@icecubepress.com
Check us out on twitter and facebook
Order direct: www.icecubepress.com

Celebrating Thirty-Three Years of Independent Publishing

To Fenna Marie—
blessed and beautiful
an even and an odd
a grand right and left